IMPROVING CRIMINAL JUSTICE REHABILITATION THROUGH THE THERAPEUTIC RELATIONSHIP

IMPROVING CRIMINAL JUSTICE REHABILITATION THROUGH THE THERAPEUTIC RELATIONSHIP

An Integrative Approach

HOWIE SCHWEBER

BLOOMSBURY ACADEMIC
NEW YORK • LONDON • OXFORD • NEW DELHI • SYDNEY

BLOOMSBURY ACADEMIC
Bloomsbury Publishing Inc, 1359 Broadway, New York, NY 10018, USA
Bloomsbury Publishing Plc, 50 Bedford Square, London, WC1B 3DP, UK
Bloomsbury Publishing Ireland, 29 Earlsfort Terrace, Dublin 2, D02 AY28, Ireland

First published in the United States of America 2026

A catalog record for this book is available from the Library of Congress.

ISBN: HB: 978-1-5381-9462-1
PB: 978-1-5381-9463-8
ePDF: 979-8-216-46744-1
eBook: 978-1-5381-9464-5

Typeset by Deanta Global Publishing Services, Chennai, India
Printed and bound in the United States of America

For product safety related questions contact productsafety@bloomsbury.com.

To find out more about our authors and books visit www.bloomsbury.com and sign up for our newsletters.

To all of my clients who have made this book possible.
To the memory of my mother Katherine, who inspired me to become a psychotherapist, and my father Seymour, who taught me that education is the wisest investment.
To my wife Susan, my daughters Katie and Lizzy, and my son-in-law Joe, whom I love more than words can tell.

CONTENTS

Introduction

As of January 25, 2021, approximately 2.2 million people were incarcerated, while another 4.5 million were on parole or probation in the United States.[1] The COVID-19 death toll continued to rise at an alarming, catastrophic rate. Earlier in the month, rioters stormed the United States Capitol, and Donald John Trump's first presidency term ended. The pandemic, economic uncertainty, climate change, exorbitant health care costs, systemic racism, political divisiveness, and racial disparity in police shootings were at the forefront of US politics and Americans' minds. On top of this, criminal justice reform advocates were fighting police brutality, mass incarceration, prison violence, inadequate housing and healthcare, long criminal sentences, court case delays, racism, discrimination, and rehabilitation issues plaguing the United States' judicial system. Against that background, I decided to begin writing this book in an attempt to provide a template for a much-needed psychological approach to increase and expedite rehabilitation for people involved in the US justice system. This book also strives to address and decrease the discrimination and mistreatment I have witnessed against those who are incarcerated, paroled, or on probation in the United States.

Will others be interested in my professional opinions, observations, and the facts related to what I witnessed and experienced in counseling men and women involved in Colorado's criminal justice system for over forty years? Can my book make a difference for people who are incarcerated, on parole, or on probation? If criminal justice professionals can treat those who are incarcerated, on parole or probation with greater empathy, concern, and respect, would it help clients shorten their sentences and reduce recidivism? Will enhanced therapeutic interaction by criminal justice professionals benefit them, those involved in the justice system, and the criminal justice system as a whole? Is it possible that the answers to these questions might be a progressive therapeutic step in needed criminal justice reform?

I grew up in northern New Jersey, in a suburb of New York City and attended Rutgers University in 1976. My mother was a small fabric store proprietor, supplied by my family's garment industry connections. Ironically, she didn't know how to sew. I admired her ability to listen, be empathetic, and truly care about her customers. It was in her shop that my deep interest in others was nurtured. Her death from cancer when I was 17 was a heartbreaking and pivotal time for me. Both her life and death laid the foundation for my passion to become a psychotherapist.

In my sophomore year at Rutgers University, I became interested in the mistreatment of individuals incarcerated in the US criminal justice system. My first criminal justice class was taught by Dr. Sol Chaneles, chairman of the Criminal Justice Department at Rutgers. Dr. Chaneles informed the class that, in lieu of taking the final exam, students had the option of proposing a class-related question and answering it. Believing this to be an easier task than taking the final, I asked Dr. Chaneles one day after class if he was serious about the offer. Dr. Chaneles sternly stared at me and responded, "Mr. Schweber, everything I say is serious. Meet me in my office tomorrow to discuss your question." Answering my own question about how those receiving police citations for driving under the influence of alcohol (DUI) understood the cause of their event turned out to be much more difficult than taking the final exam. More importantly, this led to Dr. Chaneles becoming my mentor. I took every class Dr. Chaneles taught, organized the undergraduate criminal justice internship program at Rutgers, and ultimately instructed a summer introduction to criminal justice class. Dr. Chaneles' mentorship has had an enormous influence on my life's work in psychotherapy and criminal justice.

Over my forty years as a professional counselor, I have had the privilege of providing counseling for thousands of people involved in the justice system. A year after completing my master's degree in counseling psychology at the University of Northern Colorado in 1985, I started a private practice that continues today. In 1988, I became a Colorado Certified Addiction Specialist (CAS). In my private practice, I have provided individual and couples counseling for a wide variety of people involved in the US correctional system. I became a Colorado Licensed Professional Counselor in 1989 and a Colorado Department of Corrections Approved Treatment Provider in 1996. For twenty-five years, I facilitated mental health, substance use disorder, relapse prevention, anger management, transition, and a variety of didactic therapy groups for women and men convicted of state or federal crimes who were incarcerated in Colorado halfway houses.

In early January 2021, my youngest daughter asked me about my new year resolutions, and I informed her that I hadn't really thought about it. "How about writing that book you always talked about?" she asked. I thought about it for a moment and let the idea go. "Too much work to write a book!" I thought. A few days later I took a solo hike and again pondered her question. I told and continue to tell myself that I have a therapeutic and moral obligation to share the evidence-based knowledge I have professionally accumulated over the years to attempt to improve the United States' criminal justice system. I also asked myself, "How can I address America's criminal justice system's issues in a meaningful way?" The result is this book.

The purpose of this book is to suggest an evidence-based, practical, and empathic method, called the CMC integrative approach, that can be used by all levels of criminal justice professionals to therapeutically increase and expedite client rehabilitation. The essence of this book is that rehabilitation can be improved by justice system professionals developing a healthy, therapeutic relationship with clients. The benefits of healthy relationships include increased trust, safety, communication, emotional support, and respect. I will also attempt to use facts and forty years of facilitating individual and group counseling for those who are incarcerated, on probation or parole to examine their challenging experiences in the United States' criminal justice system. My belief is this: If criminal justice professionals can be trained to interact with people involved in the justice system in a therapeutic, empathic, rational, and respectful manner, we can more efficiently and expeditiously help restore the incarcerated, paroled, and those on probation to more meaningful and successful lives while reducing recidivism.

The major topics of this book are discussed in a general manner in order for you, the reader, to receive an overview of the United States' criminal justice system, the discrimination often experienced by clients, and to learn a therapeutic approach for attempting to increase and expedite client rehabilitation. My goal is to present this overview so that we can continue to discuss the above-stated complex issues and suggest some possible solutions. I will not be addressing the youth correctional system because I have no involvement with juvenile justice, although I suspect that they experience many of the same issues I will examine in this book. This book is not intended to be a comprehensive exploration of the many important criminal justice issues. These topics deserve entire books devoted to each issue for in-depth exploration. My goal in writing this book is to take another step forward in the quest for progressive criminal justice reform.

Finally, this book was written to inform criminal justice workers and students about a straightforward therapeutic approach that includes techniques that can be easily learned and implemented by anyone. This book is not meant to be an in-depth, complicated training manual. The techniques offered are not intended to be used in a manner in which criminal justice workers tell those involved in the justice system what to do. The book strongly suggests that criminal justice workers implement techniques by generating discussion, asking questions, and sharing information in a cooperative and collaborative approach. Over the years, I have found that those involved in the justice system are more successful when they are treated in a respectful, equitable, and collaborative manner.

Definitions from the Merriam-Webster Dictionary Online Used in This Book

(except "Client" and "Relapse," which are my definitions.)

Bias: A personal and sometimes unreasoned judgment

Client: A person who is incarcerated, on probation or parole; a person involved in the US justice system

Discrimination: A prejudiced or prejudicial outlook, action or treatment

Disparity: A noticeable and usually significant difference or dissimilarity

Ethnic: of or relating to large groups of people classed according to common racial, national, tribal, religious, linguistic or cultural origin or background

Implement: transitive verb CARRY OUT, ACCOMPLISH *especially*: to give practical effort to and ensure of actual fulfillment by concrete measures

Indifference: marked by a lack of interest, enthusiasm or concern for something

Integrative: serving to integrate (1: to form, coordinate, or blend into a functioning or unified whole: unite) or favoring integration: directed toward integration

Interpersonal: being, relating to, or involving relations between persons

Latine: of, relating to, or marked by Latin American heritage

Prejudice: injury or damage resulting from some judgment or action of another in disregard of one's rights

Prosocial: *also*: relating to or promoting behavior that benefits others or society

Race: any one of the groups that humans are often divided into based on physical traits regarded as common among people of a shared ancestry

Recidivism: a tendency to relapse into a previous condition or mode of behavior *especially*: relapse into criminal behavior

Relapse: making a pledge to change a behavior and breaking that commitment

Vet, Vetted: 1. a. to evaluate for possible approval or acceptance[2]

Please note that throughout the book I have italicized my personal experiences.

1

The Characteristics of People Involved in the Justice System and Racial Disparities

As of December 31, 2022, approximately 5.4 million adults were incarcerated, on probation, or on parole in the United States.[1] This means that approximately 2 percent of all adults in the United States were under some form of correctional supervision. The average American involved in the justice system is white, male, eighteen years of age or older,[2] and nonviolent.[3] This description may be misleading due to the racial disparity and the differences in the treatment of ethnic groups that currently appear to exist in the United States' criminal justice system.

The purpose of this chapter is to discuss the demographic and psychological characteristics of those who are incarcerated, on probation or parole, and the racial disparity that currently exists in the United States' criminal justice system. Possible sociological and criminological causes of crime will be examined. The association between adverse childhood experiences (ACEs) and those involved in the justice system will also be discussed.

The *2023 Crime in the Nation* [United States] *Statistics* press release and report produced by the Federal Bureau of Investigation (FBI) indicates that the estimated number of violent crimes committed in the United States from 2023 to 2024 was 1,201,857 (homicide: 20,703; rape: 120,437; robbery: 214,935; and aggravated assault: 1,081,420). Additionally, there were an estimated 6,119,495 property crimes, including 796,483 burglaries, 4,254,880 larcenies and thefts, and 1,031,839 motor vehicle thefts that year.[4] The FBI defines violent crime in the United States as "those offenses that involve force or threat of force."[5] A 2023 Statistica, a data and business intelligence platform, article titled "Reported Violent Crime Rate in the U.S. from 1990–2020" stated that the FBI estimated violent crime in the United States in 2020 was approximately 4 percent of all crime.[6] Most people involved in the US justice system have not committed violent offenses.

Psychological Characteristics

Psychology poses the question "What are the general individual psychological characteristics of people who are involved in America's correctional system?" Another way to ask this question might be, "What causes an individual to commit a crime?" Although all people are unique, psychology attempts to diagnose individuals in the hope that psychiatrists, psychologists, licensed professional counselors, alcohol/drug and correctional counselors, and social workers will be able to establish successful treatment plans and a prognosis.

The Diagnostic and Statistical Manual of Mental Disorders, Fifth Edition, Text Revision (DSM-5-TR), published by the American Psychiatric Association, is the text used to diagnose people with psychological challenges. People in the justice system are often diagnosed using the DSM-5-TR as having antisocial personality disorder (ASPD). Often these clients also experience substance use disorders (SUD), anxiety, depression, and/or gambling issues.

The DSM-5-TR states that general personality disorder characteristics involve significant impairments that must include two of the following issues: thinking, emotional, impulse control, and/or getting along with others. The DSM-5-TR states these impairments are consistent over time, beginning in adolescence or early adulthood and not due to alcohol/drug use or medical-related issues or, in the case of ASPD, the occurrence of bipolar disorder or schizophrenia.[7]

The DSM-5-TR diagnostic criteria for ASPD are as follows:

Antisocial Personality Disorder Diagnostic Criteria

A. A pervasive pattern of disregard for and violation of the rights of others, occurring since age 15 years, as indicated by three (or more) of the following:

1. Failure to conform to social norms with respect to lawful behaviors, as indicated by repeatedly performing acts that are grounds for arrest.
2. Deceitfulness, as indicated by repeated lying, use of aliases, or conning others for personal profit or pleasure.
3. Impulsivity or failure to plan ahead.
4. Irritability and aggressiveness, as indicated by repeated physical fights or assaults.
5. Reckless disregard for safety of self or others.
6. Consistent irresponsibility, as indicated by repeated failure to sustain consistent work behavior or honor financial obligations.
7. Lack of remorse, as indicated by being indifferent to or rationalizing having hurt, mistreated, or stolen from another.

B. The individual is at least age 18 years.

C. There is evidence of conduct disorder with onset before age 15 years.

D. The occurrence of antisocial behavior is not exclusively during the course of schizophrenia or bipolar disorder.

Reprinted with permission from the Diagnostic and Statistical Manual of Mental Disorders, Fifth Edition, Text Revision (Copyright © 2022). American Psychiatric Association. All Rights Reserved.

To receive an ASPD diagnosis, the individual must be at least eighteen years old. If the above behaviors occur before the age of eighteen, the child or adolescent can be diagnosed with conduct disorder. Finally, to receive the ASPD diagnosis, the individual must have displayed conduct disorder characteristics before the age of fifteen. Basically, conduct disorder characteristics are childhood and adolescent traits similar to an ASPD diagnosis. In simpler terms, to be clinically diagnosed with ASPD, a person needs to exhibit a consistent pattern of disregard for other people that begins before the age of fifteen years old and continues into adulthood. People diagnosed with ASPD are usually characterized as being deceitful, manipulative, unlawful, dishonest, impulsive, irrational, aggressive, irresponsible, charming, unremorseful, blaming others, lacking empathy, and/or inflating their self-appraisal.

Making a diagnosis using the DSM-5-TR is a complicated process usually done by psychiatrists, psychologists, licensed professional counselors, and social workers. My goal in presenting this information is to give the reader a summary of a complex process done by mental health professionals in order to help explain how a client may receive an ASPD diagnosis.[8] Another goal is to help the reader understand the psychological characteristics of many of those involved in the US justice system. Numerous people involved in the justice system usually have moderate ASPD characteristics.

What I have discovered while having the privilege of counseling many different types of people involved in the justice system is that most are on the continuum of having ASPD. I usually find myself stating in the criminal justice system paperwork that the client exhibits ASPD characteristics, and I only occasionally diagnose someone with DSM-5-TR ASPD. There is a wide range of criminal behaviors and characteristics, and some are clearly more severe and extreme than others. Unfortunately, dramatic, violent, and heinous crimes dominate news sources, leading many to believe these represent the majority of criminal behaviors when, in fact, they are rare. Most people in the correctional system have been convicted of nonviolent crimes and exhibit a moderate amount of ASPD characteristics.

Another glaring issue that those under US correctional system supervision experience involves alcohol and/or drug SUD. A 2010 National Center on Addiction and Substance Abuse (CASA) at Columbia University report states that 65 percent of the United States' prison population met the DSM-IV criteria for alcohol or other drug abuse and addiction diagnosis.[9] Another 20 percent did not meet the DSM-IV criteria for a SUD yet their criminal behavior was associated with alcohol and/or drugs (e.g., intoxicated while committing a crime; committed a crime to secure money to purchase illegal drugs). The bottom line is that the above-stated report indicates 85 percent of the United States' prison population may also have drug/alcohol-related issues.

Sociological and Criminological Considerations

According to the American Sociological Association, "Sociology is the study of social life, social change, and the social causes and consequences of human behavior."[10] Criminology is seen by some as a subfield of sociology and by others as a distinct discipline joined together with sociology in an attempt to answer the challenging questions, "What are the societal causes of crime?" and "How does social disorganization affect criminal behavior?" Another intriguing question is, "Do individuals learn criminal behavior when associating with other people involved in the justice system?" *Often, my clients under correctional system supervision inform me that they have become or will learn to be more successful criminals when incarcerated and associating with other imprisoned people.* Sociology and criminology examine how social disorder, inadequate parenting, poverty, neighborhoods, communities, schools, peer groups, and dysfunctional family systems affect the individual or group. Criminology also considers the individual's psychological characteristics that may contribute to their antisocial behavior. I have found that it is crucial, when assessing an individual, to seriously consider all of the above-stated sociological factors that may contribute to their involvement in the justice system.

Adverse Childhood Experiences (ACEs)

Adverse Childhood Experiences, also known by the acronym **ACEs**, are possible traumatic and stressful incidents that occur in a person's childhood. ACEs can cause a child to experience instability and not feel safe. It can be strongly argued that stability and safety are essential in a child's development. Childhood is usually considered to be the time frame starting from a person's birth and ending at 17 years and 364 days of age. **Psychological trauma** can be defined as an experience of significant fear and difficulty, and/or the emotional reaction to that incident. A 1995–7 Centers for Disease Control and Prevention (CDC) and Kaiser Permanente California study found that children who experience physical, sexual, and emotional abuse and neglect, household violence, and other mental health and stability-related issues, either directly or by interacting with household members, have higher incidences of physical health and psychological issues during adolescence and adulthood.

There are three categories of ACEs. These categories are Abuse, Neglect, and Household Dysfunction. There are a total of ten ACEs that fall under these three categories.

- **Abuse**
  - Physical
  - Emotional
  - Sexual
- **Neglect**
  - Physical
  - Emotional
- **Household Dysfunction includes a household member . . .**
  - having a mental illness
  - being treated violently
  - being incarcerated
  - having SUD characteristics
  - experiencing a separation and/or a divorce

Other ACEs that are recognized yet not included in the list above are: being bullied, poverty, racism, being unhoused, and violence in the community.

ACEs research results include the significant findings of the 1995–7 CDC and Kaiser study as well as many associated studies. The significant findings of these studies are that more than 66 percent of the US population, regardless of their socioeconomic status, report experiencing one ACE. Approximately 25 percent of the population reported experiencing three or more ACEs. **The findings of these studies also concluded that the greater the number of ACEs that a child experiences, the increased likelihood of their having physical and mental health issues in adolescence and adulthood.** ACEs have been connected to chronic physical health issues including diabetes, heart disease, cancer, blood pressure, and skin diseases. ACEs have also been associated with psychological issues including SUDs, mental illness, anxiety, and depression.

The phrase "**toxic stress,**" created by The National Scientific Council on the Developing Child, describes the overactivation of the human stress response (fight-flight-freeze-fawn [flatter]) and its negative effects on a child's developing brain, immune system, and heart, as well as other physiological systems. Multiple ACE incidents experienced over a longer period of time trigger an excessive stress response. The continuation of this process can cause lasting stress reactions that may negatively affect a child's physiological and psychological development. When the human body recognizes a significant threat, the fight-flight-freeze-fawn automatic physiological response occurs, possibly increasing anxiety, heart rate, adrenaline, cortisol, and sweating, among other physical symptoms. This allows people to fight, flee, freeze, or fawn in a threatening situation as a survival response. Over an extended period of time, toxic stress is the result of the overused flight, fight, freeze or fawn response and can have serious negative long-term effects on the human body. In other words, when a child is in an ongoing, tension-filled situation that causes repeated and lengthy flight, fight, freeze or fawn responses, toxic stress can be the result. Thus, children who have ACEs and toxic stress over a longer period of time are more prone to have physical and psychological health consequences in adolescence and adulthood.[11, 12]

The Compassion Prison Project (CPP) is a nonprofit, grassroots organization committed to creating trauma-informed prisons through education and training. The CPP's work focuses on how trauma can affect people who are incarcerated or working in prison. According to The Compassion Prison Project's website, 64 percent of the US population has experienced one ACE as compared to 98 percent of the United States' prison population. The CPP has developed "Trauma Talks," a sixteen-part video and workbook curriculum for those who are living in prison. The goal of the "Trauma Talks" program is to help those who are incarcerated learn about their traumas to better control their nervous system and ultimately maintain a prosocial lifestyle. CPP also offers an eight-part Correctional Officer (CO) Trauma-Responsive Training course designed to educate COs about how trauma affects a person's physical and mental health. This training also discusses how COs can create a safe correctional environment in which they, and those involved in the justice system can build trust and collaborate. Finally, this training addresses ways in which COs can engage in healthy, therapeutic self-care activities.[13]

Left untreated, trauma may result in an individual's increased likelihood of becoming involved in the justice system. ACEs seem to cause people to experience psychological challenges, physiological issues, inadequate decision-making, and poor impulse control. Also, it appears that client trauma is often ignored by justice system employees. Those involved with the justice system with untreated trauma may be at an increased risk of recidivating. If an individual's trauma can be addressed via empathy and appropriate mental health referral and treatment, individuals may have a better chance to adequately address their trauma in a healthy manner.

ACE-related research indicates that most people involved in the US justice system have encountered ACEs. It appears that the more ACEs a person has experienced, the greater their likelihood of being involved in the justice system. In one study mentioned in a 2022 article cited by The Urban Institute, a nonprofit research organization, men who had committed crimes experienced almost four times as many ACEs as the average adult male.[14] This article went on to discuss how helping parents and caregivers learn how to create a safe and healthy living environment for children may decrease ACEs. The article states that this can be accomplished through parenting classes, trauma information and education, mental health counseling, and nurse home visits, to name a few possible solutions. Adults who have encountered ACEs may benefit from psychological counseling, exercise, diet, nutrition, adequate sleep, healthy socializing, and self-care. If correctional professionals can recognize that those involved in the justice system have most likely experienced ACEs, it may help both groups heal and clients pursue prosocial lifestyles.

Racial Disparities

The National Conference of State Legislatures (NCSL) is a bipartisan political organization advocating for states' interests and supporting legislators. In an online article updated on May 24, 2022, the NCSL stated that "people of color are far more likely to enter the nation's justice system than the general population."[15] The Sentencing Project,[16] Urban Institute,[17] and Vera Institute of Justice[18] are all national organizations that refer to evidence-based research suggesting there are racial disparities in the United States' criminal justice system. These studies provide evidence that African Americans or Blacks are more likely to be stopped by police, arrested, convicted, and receive longer prison sentences than whites. Latines and Blacks have a significantly higher likelihood of being incarcerated in their lifetime than whites. These various factors contribute to the disproportionately high rate of persons of color in the criminal justice system.

The racial disparity that exists in the US criminal justice system is revealed by statistical data. In July 2024, the United States Census Bureau estimated that the US population is 340,110,988 and 58.4 percent white, 19.5 percent Hispanic or Latine, 13.7 percent African American or Black, 6.4 percent Asian, 1.3 percent American Indian and Alaskan Native, and 0.3 percent Native Hawaiian and Other Pacific Islander.[19] The most current FBI estimates of arrests according to race that I was able to locate are from the *2023 Crime in the Nation Statistics* press release and report, which lists racial arrests in 2023 as 64 percent white, 29 percent Black or African American, 2 percent American Indian or Alaskan Native, 1 percent Asian, less than 1 percent Native Hawaiian or Other Pacific Islander, and 3 percent unknown.[20] This report does not separate out Latine or Hispanic ethnicities from Caucasians since Latine is defined as an ethnicity and not a race (see Introduction, Definitions). Many states do not differentiate Latine or Hispanic ethnicity from all white arrests.[21] The FBI's *2019 Crime in the United States*, Table 43A, includes a separate category which indicates that Latine and Hispanic people were arrested for 19.1 percent of crimes in 2019 and has a footnote stating, "The ethnicity totals are representative of those agencies that provided ethnicity breakdowns. Not all agencies provide ethnicity data; therefore, the race and ethnicity totals will not equal."[22] A 2021 Pew Research Article states that 58 percent of Hispanics identify their race as white.[23] **If we speculate that the white arrests listed in the FBI's *2023 Crime in the Nation Statistics* report include at least some Latine and Hispanic people who do not identify themselves as white, we can make an educated guess that white people actually make up less than the 64% of the 2023 arrests reported. We can also speculate the number of Latine and Hispanic arrests may be underreported because not all criminal justice agencies differentiate Hispanics and Latine from white arrests.** A Bureau of Justice Statistics (United States) preliminary data report dated September 2023 indicated that as of December 31, 2021, the US prison population (not including local jails) according to race and ethnicity were 32 percent Black or African American, 31 percent white, 23 percent Hispanic or Latine, 10 percent multiracial or other race, 2 percent American Indian or Alaskan Native, and 1 percent Asian, Native Hawaiian, or Other Pacific Islander.[24]

These estimated statistics reveal the racial disparity found in the United States' criminal justice system. All things being equal, we would hope to see the United States' Census Bureau race percentages being approximately equivalent to the race percentages of those individuals who are arrested each year in the United States. In this example, we are comparing the estimated U.S. Census Bureau statistics of July 2024 to the most up-to-date, 2023 FBI arrests according to race. The US Census is produced every ten years.[25] Even though we are comparing different years, I am using this example to attempt to provide the most accurate, approximate, current picture of racial disparity that exists in the US justice system. Hispanic and Latine people make up 19.5 percent of the United States' population and most likely account for *at least* 19.1 percent of people who are arrested in the United States each year. Hispanic and Latine arrests are most likely underreported due to the above-stated issues. African Americans or Blacks make up 13.7 percent of the United States' population and 29 percent of people who are detained in legal custody. American Indians and Alaskan Natives make up 1.3 percent of the United States' population and 2 percent of those who are arrested in the US justice system. These statistics suggest that African American and Black, American Indian and Alaskan Native, and most likely Hispanic and Latine people are all overrepresented in the US criminal justice system, illuminating the racial disparity found in this network.

There are many facts and theories associated with the causes of the racial disparity that exists in the US criminal justice system. It is not in the scope of this book to try to thoroughly answer the difficult question of what actually brings about this racial disparity. **Possible causes appear to be unconscious bias by justice system workers**, such as racial profiling, which is based on stereotypical assumptions associated with a person's race, color, or ethnicity; **socioeconomic inequality**, including poverty, which disproportionately affects minority communities; **and racism** in the form of discriminatory laws and actions. The best book I have read on the subject is *The New Jim Crow* by Michelle Alexander.[26] This book suggests that the United States' justice system is being used as a mechanism to discriminate against African Americans.

If criminal justice professionals can learn to treat all clients equally, therapeutically, and professionally, I believe the justice system can decrease discrimination and recidivism, improve rehabilitation efforts, and help clients lead more successful lives.

Conclusion

In summary, most of the people under correctional system supervision whom I have seen in individual/group counseling have been either white (approximately 50 percent); or African American or Black, Hispanic or Latine, or Asian or Native American (approximately 50 percent). They usually have been convicted of nonviolent offenses and have moderate ASPD characteristics (unlawful behavior, episodic dishonesty, impulsivity, poor anger management, low empathy, irresponsibility, limited self-awareness, and low levels of guilt). These clients usually exhibit alcohol and/or drug SUD characteristics, episodic irrational thinking, and inadequate decision-making and problem-solving skills. Sociological considerations including an individual's socioeconomic status, inadequate parenting, peer groups, neighborhood, and dysfunctional family system may also be contributing factors to a person's involvement in the US justice system. Finally, most people involved in the justice system have encountered traumatic ACEs.

ASPD and SUD are complicated and challenging to treat successfully.[27, 28] Each disorder, in itself, presents major challenges to clients and clinicians. Prognoses, the forecast of the likely outcome of treating individuals with these issues, are generally not good. Recidivism rates for those involved in the justice system are high. Relapse and recurrence rates for those with SUDs and involved in the justice system are also very high. Those under the United States' correctional system supervision often exhibit both ASPD and SUD characteristics, have a poor prognosis and personalities that are not immediately engaging with those who want to help them.

It has been my professional experience that *when I have utilized the CMC integrative approach (which will be thoroughly discussed in Chapter 6), incorporating therapeutic relationship-oriented, client-centered, motivational interviewing and cognitive behavioral therapies, clients with ASPD and/or SUD have had higher success rates than the average.* These therapies are evidence-based and supported by a large amount of scientific research. Combining and implementing these therapies appears to increase the likelihood of clients receiving the treatment and learning the techniques necessary to live successful lives.

If criminal justice workers can be appropriately vetted and taught the CMC integrative approach, it could greatly benefit them and enormously enhance our ability to help those involved in the justice system. This would help criminal justice workers develop a healthier and more healing process of communication among themselves and with clients. Criminal justice workers implementing the CMC integrative approach may experience increased job satisfaction and improved self-esteem associated with higher client success rates. The majority of people involved in the justice system appear to have the interest and capacity for learning self-insight, rational thinking, and prosocial skills. Through exposure to criminal justice staff who have been given some basic education in an effective, relationship-building, motivational, and problem-solving approach, many clients may be able to complete their sentence more expeditiously, reduce their likelihood of returning to incarceration after successful sentence completion, and establish successful lives.

2

The US Criminal Justice System and Associated Issues Defined

Criminal justice is defined by the International Student as "The system through which crimes and criminals are identified, apprehended, judged and punished."[1] The overall goal of the United States' criminal justice system is to reduce crime in the community and help clients develop a prosocial, successful lifestyle.[2]

The criminal justice system consists of three branches: the police, the courts, and corrections. The police have the responsibility of enforcing the law, arresting suspected criminals, preventing crime, and protecting/serving the public. The courts' duties include ensuring that crime suspects receive a fair legal trial and determining if the alleged defendant is guilty or innocent. The correctional system's responsibilities include punishment, protecting the public from criminal behavior, and helping those involved in the justice system develop a prosocial (moral) lifestyle by teaching them therapeutic life skills.

The purpose of this chapter is to understand the basics of the US criminal justice system and the people involved with it. Issues regarding client discrimination and a general examination of the police, courts and corrections will be discussed. *In this chapter, I will also share some of my personal experiences arising from my forty years of serving as a psychotherapist associated with the corrections system.* I also invite you, the reader, to think about your own thoughts, feelings, behaviors, and experiences associated with the criminal justice system.

The Police

In the United States, the responsibility of the police is to maintain a safe and peaceful environment. Police and peace officers are defined by Dictionary.com as "an organized civil force for maintaining order, preventing and detecting crime, and enforcing the laws."[3] The responsibilities of the police include addressing crime in society, providing general emergency services, and promoting public safety by maintaining a feeling of security in communities. Police control crime by upholding the rule of law, investigating criminal behavior, and apprehending suspects. People usually contact the police when any type of individual or community emergency occurs, and they don't know who else to contact. The police maintain public order and peace by attempting to control crowds, traffic, and domestic disputes.

Multiple instances of racial bias and discrimination in the US police system have been documented in recent years, especially regarding police searches and stops.[4] In a study of almost 100 million traffic stops by police across the United States between 2011 and 2018, persons of color were more likely than Caucasians to be pulled over and searched. As the sun sets, persons of color are less likely to be stopped than in the daytime, when it is more difficult to see one's race,[5] suggesting racial bias. Similar findings have been reported in other studies. For example, a research study done in Springfield, MO, from 2012 to 2016, indicated that the average percentage of police-related traffic stops of African Americans exceeded their percentage of the driving age population.[6]

The police have the right to use force when necessary to make an arrest, maintain order, or keep the peace. **Police brutality** occurs when a member of the police department uses excessive force and violates the law.[7] Rhonda Hill, a criminal defense attorney in Chicago, Illinois, wrote in her 2017 Criminal Defense Blog that police brutality is an issue that is more common than it appears. Hill's blog states that there are five types of police brutality: "1) Excessive use of force; 2) Wrongful search and seizure; 3) Racial discrimination; 4) False arrest and wrongful imprisonment; and 5) Sexual harassment and abuse."[8] Rhonda Hill emphasized that police brutality occurs quite frequently.

According to the Nature news feature article titled "What the Data Say About Police Brutality and Racial Bias—and Which Reforms Might Work," dated June 19, 2020, by Lynne Peoples, approximately 1,000 people a year are killed by law enforcement officers in the United States.[9] The article cites several additional studies including a 2019 report which indicated that Black men are 2.5 times more likely than white men to be killed by police.[10] In another study cited by this article, African Americans who were killed by police were two times more likely than whites to be unarmed.[11]

What can be done to combat the United States' police discrimination and brutality issues? An American Psychological Association (APA) cover story "What works to reduce police brutality?" dated October 1, 2020, by Zara Abrams gave suggestions for police reform. This APA article recommended that community policing, banning chokeholds and strangleholds, crisis intervention teams, increasing mental health professionals in law enforcement agencies, and police data collection and research could possibly decrease police brutality.[12] Banning knee neck holds in all states, which apparently caused George Floyd's death, may also help decrease police brutality. In a Live Science article titled "How to Actually Stop Police Brutality According to Science" by Stephanie Pappas, dated June 4, 2020, the author uses evidence-based data to make similar recommendations. Ms. Pappas suggests that tracking police issues with data collection, demilitarizing the police (police can receive equipment from the US military), limiting police use of force, investing in alternatives (mental health treatment teams), and civilian watchdog oversight reduce police use of excessive force.[13] Training police to utilize psychological de-escalation techniques with appropriate clients as well as themselves (time-outs, deep breathing, increased assertive communication) may also reduce police use of excessive force.

A Proceedings of the National Academy of Sciences of the United States of America (PNAS) article titled "**Procedural Justice Training Reduces Police Use of Force and Complaints Against Officers**," written on May 5, 2020, and authored by G. Wood, T. Tyler, and A. Papachristos provides additional evidence-based research on how to decrease police use of excessive force. This paper states, "**The procedural justice model of policing, which emphasizes transparency, explaining policing actions, and responding to community concerns, has been identified as a strategy for decreasing the number of interactions in which civilians experience disrespectful treatment or the unjustified use of force.**" This research showed that when police respectfully communicate and interact with community members before making decisions, they reduce the number of civilian complaints and the use of force.[14] Transparency will apparently decrease the public's current growing distrust of the police.

It is important to note that clients may have constructive or negative interactions with the police which can respectively result in positive, as well as challenging outcomes. *I have had limited personal interactions with the police which have brought about mostly positive, and occasionally challenging results. Like most people, my police interactions have been for emergencies and traffic violations. My police encounters were mostly helpful and respectful, and occasionally anxiety-producing and intimidating.* It appears to be important for justice system staff to empathize with clients in regard to their police encounters in order to help support their rehabilitation efforts.

Police appear to be the most helpful to society when they function as an active part of the community, address crime, and provide a safe environment for citizens. Communities seem to benefit when police build trust with them through collaborative and considerate interactions. **It appears that police can be most helpful to society when they are interacting in a professional, ethical, empathic, transparent, accountable, and community-building manner.**

The Courts

The US court system is structured in a hierarchical manner. On the federal level, there are ninety-four district courts that hear civil and criminal cases involving federal law or a constitutional issue. There are thirteen federal appeal courts that can hear an appeal from a federal district court's decision. There is one Supreme Court that has jurisdiction over all federal court cases and issues decided by state supreme courts on the basis of federal law.[15] **Less than ten percent of all legal cases are federal.**[16]

Every US state's constitution and laws create their own court system. This court system hears and rules on all legal cases that are state related. Each state has trial courts that are civil and criminal. If one is challenging a state court's decision, they do so in the state's appellate courts. The state's highest court rules on appeals from the state's appellate courts.[17] For the purpose of this discussion, we will focus on federal and state criminal courts and their associated personnel. These include judges, district or prosecuting attorneys, public defenders or defense attorneys, courtroom staff, and law enforcement personnel assigned to the court.

I have provided individual and group counseling for clients convicted of federal and state crimes in Boulder and Denver, Colorado. I was granted a federal contract to provide individual mental health counseling for qualified federal clients in Boulder County, Colorado, beginning in the mid 1990s. Under this contract, a federal client needed to meet the following qualifications for me to provide psychotherapy: committed a federal offense, living in Boulder County, and in need of mental health counseling. These criteria limited the number of federal clients I counseled. The clients I provided counseling for were convicted of crimes including tax evasion, embezzlement, counterfeiting money, US mail tampering, flying misconduct, interstate and intercountry drug trafficking, and illegal behavior in Rocky Mountain National Park. I found these cases extremely interesting because of their uniqueness.

Federal and state criminal courts address, process, and settle legal disputes. They are the places where Americans hope justice will be served. Prosecuting attorneys and defense lawyers present circumstantial and factual evidence arguing their respective cases, and guilty or not guilty verdicts are reached. Cases are decided based on the individual(s) who offer the most rational arguments built on facts and the law.

Although complicated by federal and individual state rules, the criminal justice court process, in general, follows a basic procedure that can include the following steps:

1. **Investigation** of a possible crime by the police: The police need "probable cause" (a reason to believe, or evidence, that a crime has been committed) to proceed with their criminal case.
2. **Arrest** of the alleged defendant based on probable cause.
3. **Prosecution** (formally charging) by a district attorney (DA), who works for the federal government or the state: The DA will proceed to prosecute an alleged client based on the seriousness of the possible crime and the evidence or
4. **Indictment** by a grand jury or filing of "information" by the prosecuting attorney (DA): In many states and the federal

government, a grand jury (which can consist of twelve to twenty-three and usually has sixteen to twenty-three jurors) decides to bring criminal charges (an indictment) against a person in a hearing that is only attended by the prosecutor, judge, and jury. An indictment, or formally charging the alleged client, is based on probable cause. In other states, a prosecutor files "information" (complaint) to officially charge the defendant. Then a preliminary hearing, attended by the defendant, is held to discover if the evidence is strong enough to pursue criminal charges.

5. **Arraignment**: Before the trial begins, a defendant has this court date to plead either guilty or not.
6. **Bail** and/or pretrial detention: Bail is a security (usually money), determined by the judge and paid by the defendant, to ensure they will attend a trial. Pretrial detention is a term of temporary confinement (incarceration) before a defendant goes to trial if the defendant is denied bail.
7. **Preliminary Hearing** by a judge: This is the first trial in which the judge hears the probable cause evidence that is usually presented by the prosecuting lawyer against the defendant, and the defense attorney can argue. A defendant can waive their right to this procedure and proceed with their criminal court process.
8. **Plea Bargain**: An agreement between the prosecuting lawyer and defense attorney resulting in the defendant pleading guilty in order to receive a reduced criminal sentence. Approximately 94% of all criminal convictions are the result of plea bargains.[18]
9. **Trial**: The legal dispute is addressed, processed by a prosecuting and a defense attorney, and resolved by a judge or jury in a criminal court.

10. **Sentencing** by the judge: the legal consequence when one is found guilty of committing a crime.
11. **Appeal**: a request for a higher court to consider changing a legal decision.
12. **Punishment**: The penalty for being convicted of a crime (e.g., loss of a privilege, fine, probation, home confinement, community corrections, incarceration, etc.).[19, 20]

In my forty years of counseling people involved in the justice system, I have been subpoenaed to testify in court a handful of times. The judge is seated at a much higher level than everyone else, looking down on the courtroom, surrounded by large walls and symbols of justice. This creates an environment that can feel intimidating. I have mostly attended state courtrooms, where the environment feels quite intimidating, yet less so than federal courts. Although the state courtrooms appear large, they are a smaller version of their federal counterparts. My testimony has included informing judges about domestic violence, answering questions about the possible mental health issues a client may be experiencing, or handing over a client's psychological chart when court-ordered to do so. I was once subpoenaed to appear with a client's psychological chart as it was believed this person had confessed to a cellmate that he had committed a heinous crime. My client never informed me about any such thing, yet I still had to appear in court. I attended court and informed the judge of the above-stated information, attempting to protect my client's right to privacy. Psychotherapists work hard to establish a therapeutic alliance to build trust, and hopefully have clients experience some healing emotional catharses associated with past traumas. Despite my objection, the judge ordered me to hand over the client's chart. Given the potential for a courtroom to feel intimidating, I believe that it is important for attorneys, judges, and other courtroom personnel to take people's emotional experiences into account and treat defendants and witnesses empathically, and with dignity and respect.

It is important to note that when interfacing with the legal court system, psychologists, psychotherapists, social workers, professional counselors, wardens, supervisors, administrators, and others working in the criminal justice system may need to be familiar with and adhere to federal, state and local laws. These laws are specific to the federal government and each state. Federal laws apply to all people in the United States, whether they are citizens or not. State and local laws apply to all people who visit, are employed, live, and/or commit a crime in a specific state, whether they are US citizens or not. Additionally, each profession, such as licensed professional counselors (LPCs), has its own guidelines. For example, a licensed professional counselor working in Colorado has an obligation to be familiar with the Colorado LPC guidelines as well as the state and local laws when interacting with the court system.

Federal, state and local laws, and professional guidelines regarding the US criminal justice system and clients can be complex. Thus, a justice system professional or staff member can benefit from consulting with a clinical consultant or supervisor, and/or a lawyer when interacting with the legal court system. *In my forty years of private practice and twenty-five years of facilitating individual and group counseling in Colorado justice system halfway houses, I have always maintained a clinical consultant and met with them regularly. I have always worked with consultants who have more experience than I do, making them mentors as well as supervisors, which I value and appreciate. As a member of the American Counseling Association (ACA), I have had access to general information about the law which I utilize when necessary, especially when more complex justice system-related situations occur. I have found clinical consultants and ACA assistance invaluable in my career.* It is also extremely important for justice system workers to document in writing client interactions according to their professional guidelines for legal purposes. Areas that are governed by laws and professional guidelines may include, yet may not be limited to:

1. **Mandated Reporting** that establishes when professionals and staff are required to report suicide, homicide, child or at-risk adult abuse/neglect-related incidents, court-ordered information, and threats to

national security to the police, courts, and/or social services/child protection.

2. **Psychotherapist–Client Privileged Communication** including the circumstances that dictate when privileged communication and client confidentiality apply and when a person involved in the justice system's privacy is or is not protected by law.
3. **How and When to Respond to Subpoenas**—laws that indicate if and when a justice system worker has to appear in court and whether or not to submit client chart information.
4. **Expert Witness Status** including which justice system professionals and staff summoned to court can be considered to be expert witnesses.

Justice system professionals and staff are responsible for knowing applicable federal, state and local laws and professional guidelines. Consultants, supervisors, administrators, professional organizations, and lawyers can help justice system employees understand these sometimes complex laws and guidelines.[21]

Plea bargaining, the agreement between a prosecuting and defense attorney resulting in the defendant pleading guilty for a supposed reduced criminal sentence, expedites the clogged courtroom process yet at an unknown expense to the criminal justice and court system in general, and the defendant in particular. When seeking evidence-based research on plea bargaining, it becomes clear that little exists. According to an article produced in 2020 by The Vera Institute of Justice, an independent, nonprofit, national research organization, "Ultimately, the lack of clarity regarding the administration and impacts of plea bargaining is perhaps the most important thing that research has revealed." The article suggests that plea bargaining may be contributing to the United States' mass incarceration and systemic racism issues.[22] It appears evident that future research concerning the effects of plea bargaining on the justice system, defendant, and society in general is essential.

Multiple court-related issues may be seen as hindering the United States' criminal justice system. Politics, wealth advantages, courtroom environment, intimidation, courts being backed up, public defenders experiencing high caseloads, and plea bargaining are only some of these issues. Future research concerning these issues may help create a more successful court system.

Corrections

The United States' justice "corrections" system is a catch-all phrase that describes a variety of private and governmental organizations that punish, supervise and provide treatment for those convicted of a criminal offense.[23] Corrections implements sentencing orders of the criminal courts. The United States' corrections system includes prisons, jails, halfway houses, work release, electronic monitoring, probation, parole, restitution, fines, community service and restorative justice. Each of these is described below.

Prisons, also known as penitentiaries or correctional facilities, are "institutions designed for the confinement of convicted felons who have been sentenced to more than one year of incarceration."[24] Prisons are run by the Federal Bureau of Prisons or a state's department of corrections (DOC).

A **jail** is defined as "a building designated or regularly used for confinement of individuals who are sentenced for minor crimes or who are unable to gain release on bail and are currently awaiting trial."[25] Jails are correctional facilities located in a client's city or county for people usually serving less than a one-year sentence.

Criminal **halfway houses** are correctional, community-based facilities providing a structured, supervised environment for those involved in the justice system. Halfway houses require clients to follow rules and regulations and attempt to help them reintegrate into society. Clients gain privileges for compliant behavior and are rewarded by being allowed to attain gainful employment, visit with family and friends, and shop for necessities. Halfway house residents are usually required to attend cognitive behavioral offense-specific and/or substance use treatment. They allow clients to have a lifestyle halfway between jail and independence. Halfway house residents may be directly sentenced for less serious crimes or DOC or federal clients progressing from prison or jail and successfully working toward completing their sentence. Halfway house residents are often responsible for paying for their own rent and treatment.

Criminal **work release** programs are a form of corrections that allow a person involved in the justice system to leave an incarceration situation (e.g., jail, halfway house) unescorted to attend work. The client has the responsibility to return to their work release incarceration program when their employment shift is complete. The benefits of work release are that the client is allowed to engage in a therapeutic employment situation and transition back into the community.

Electronic Monitoring is "the use of an electronic device that is fastened to a person, animal, or object, so that police, scientists, or other people can know where they are." Electronic monitoring allows the client to not be incarcerated, or to be released early from jail and to be a part of their community.[26] Clients on electronic monitoring maintain living situations outside of the justice system.

Parole is the early release from incarceration of a usually compliant person who is in the process of completing her/his sentence. The client is supervised by a correctional officer and agrees to abide by parole rules and regulations. If the client does not comply with their parole conditions, they may be required to resume their incarceration.

Probation is a legal ruling usually given as an alternative to jail or prison, or in which a client is released from incarceration before their sentence is complete to help them reintegrate into society. The person is usually supervised by a correctional officer and agrees to abide by probation rules and regulations. If the client fails to comply with probation rules, they may be regressed from probation and required to return to court to receive a more severe legal sentence.

Bail is an amount of money or property a defendant must pay to be released from incarceration before their trial. Bail ensures the alleged defendant will appear at their trial. If they don't, the defendant loses their bail. Bail is returned when the trial is over. Bail allows for the release of the defendant with the promise they will appear in court.[27]

Restitution is the legal requirement of a person involved in the justice system to repay money or perform community service (similar to volunteer work) to the victim or society.[28]

Fines are "monetary charges imposed upon individuals who have been convicted of a crime or a lesser offense."[29]

Restorative Justice is "a philosophical framework and a series of programs for the criminal justice system that emphasize the need to repair the harm done to crime victims through a process of negotiation, mediation, victim empowerment and reparation."[30] Restorative Justice focuses on the needs of the crime victim, person involved in the justice system, and community, and seeks resolution of issues through problem-solving communication between all parties. A person's antisocial behavior is understood as a violation of people and/or relationships. Restorative Justice theory promotes the belief that positive outcomes are more likely to occur if the perpetrator and victim can therapeutically communicate (if all parties involved feel safe and secure about discussing the issue at hand) using conflict resolution techniques (see Chapter 6, "7. Anger Management").

I have facilitated counseling for twenty-five years in halfway houses, worked with many different criminal justice system employees, and observed two types of professionals: "authoritarians" and "relationship-builders." The authoritarians can tend to exhibit a military-style attitude, including a very structured, non-emotional, and seemingly condescending approach towards clients. I noticed authoritarians sometimes threatening clients with write-ups for minor violations and ordering them to their rooms when overwhelmed, whether the client deserved the punishment or not. I would announce groups starting at the halfway house on a loudspeaker and call all the clients in the group "Mr." so and so to summon them to attend. I was once told by an authoritarian line staff worker that staff were instructed to call all inmates by their last name only. This is an example of a corrections rule apparently designed to support a military environment to help control clients' behavior. Clients can interpret last name identification as authoritarian and impersonal. The relationship-builders have interacted with clients in a more considerate, somewhat empathic, and helpful manner. I have observed them listening and treating clients in a caring way, making their lives a bit more manageable while in the halfway house. I perceived the halfway house relationship-building staff as being more supportive of client rehabilitation efforts. Related research, which will be discussed in the section "Correctional Officer Typologies" in Chapter 3, also confirms relationship-building skills seem to produce more positive client rehabilitation outcomes.

Today's US prisons have multiple problems, motivating more and more interested people, as well as criminal justice professionals, to investigate what is occurring in these institutions. These problems have been the catalyst for a growing criminal justice reform movement. In a 2018 article produced by The Vera Institute titled "Examining Prisons Today," the authors document how the United States' prison problems include violence, inadequate medical care, mass incarceration, overcrowding, isolation, poor building conditions, physical and sexual assault by correctional staff or other clients, neglect of providing basic human necessities, solitary confinement's negative psychological effects, and the post-traumatic stress disorder (PTSD) experienced by clients when they leave prison.[31] The United States' prisons also fall short in providing adequate mental health services for clients.[32] In a Marshall Project article titled "Job Opening: No Training, Low Pay, High Turnover" dated June 5, 2015, evidence is provided documenting correctional officers' inadequate training, understaffing, low pay, and high job turnover rates.[33]

Although persons involved in the justice system can exhibit serious disruptive, problematic, and violent behavior in correctional settings, the majority are nonviolent and can respond well to loss of privilege discipline. In my years of professional experience as a counselor, I have observed that an authoritarian, overly structured, punitive attitude displayed by justice system staff tends to be less effective in helping clients establish a prosocial, healthy lifestyle as compared to the more empathic "relationship-building" approach.

Conclusion

The US criminal justice system includes the police, courts and corrections. Each of these entities is an organization within itself, and they are interrelated in an attempt to create a fair legal process to apprehend, judge, punish, and psychologically treat people involved in the justice system. Together, these entities serve the purpose of protecting society, ensuring people are judged fairly, and helping those involved in the justice system to develop successful lifestyles. I am hopeful that sharing my personal and professional experiences with the police, courts and corrections motivates you, the reader, to think about your own interactions with the criminal justice system. While the police, courts and corrections have been generally successful, this chapter has also highlighted several of the problems exhibited within each division. It is beyond the scope of this book to resolve the many issues that have been currently identified in the US criminal justice system. I am suggesting that if we recognize these issues, we can generate increased thought and discussion about how the US criminal justice system can continue to make progress in developing more effective therapeutic client approaches. This, in turn, may decrease recidivism for those involved in the justice system and improve client rehabilitation and criminal justice worker employment success and satisfaction.

3

Correctional Officer Types, Psychological Reactance, and How People Change

It seems essential to understand the general personality characteristics of US justice system workers and those who are incarcerated, on probation or parole in order to improve their interaction with each other and client rehabilitation. Working in the criminal justice system is usually stressful due to challenging physical correctional environments, clients, and violence-related issues. The clashing of personality characteristics between justice workers and those involved in the system may impede the rehabilitation of clients.

Correctional officer (CO) typologies (personality types) affect the way they interact with people involved in the justice system. Those under correctional supervision can also have challenging personality characteristics, already discussed (see Chapter 1, "Psychological Characteristics"), which can hinder their progression through the justice system. Psychological reactance, as discussed below, explains how those under correctional supervision may not be amenable to a justice system worker's commands, instructions, unsolicited advice, and/or client requested suggestions. Improving CO and client interactions and understanding psychological reactance and The Stages of Change can help justice system workers therapeutically support clients. This information may help clients better recognize their readiness to make thought and behavioral changes in order to establish a more prosocial lifestyle.

Correctional Officer Typologies

I have only been able to find limited data on the typology, or personality types, of the many groups of people who work in the criminal justice system. Most of the research I found focused on COs. It is my belief that COs, parole, probation, and pretrial officers, case managers, and line staff have the most frequent interactions with clients convicted of a crime. CO's responsibilities, according to CorrectionalOfficer.org, are to enforce rules, keep order, supervise activities, search for contraband, inspect facilities to ensure they meet standards, report on client conduct, and aid in the rehabilitation and counseling of those who are incarcerated.[1] A research study produced by Mary Ann Farkas in 2000, in which she interviewed seventy-nine COs, found that COs she classified as "rule enforcers," "hard liners," and "loners" enforced the standard correctional rules, goals, and values. Farkas labeled other COs as "people workers" and "synthetic officers," who were found to incorporate their own values and manners when performing their jobs.[2]

In the 2017 book titled *American Prisons and Jails: An Encyclopedia of Controversies and Trends*, by Megan M. King and Ryan M. Labrecque, the authors state that CO typology research indicates there are five types of COs: true carers, limited carers, old school, conflicted, and damaged. True carers are defined as supportive and genuinely concerned about people involved in the justice system. They encourage clients to be prosocial and use communication skills to build relationships. Limited carers express concern about clients, follow institutional rules, and make slight adjustments (depending on the situation) usually supporting clients. Old schoolers are strict institutional rule enforcers. They will address a client's needs if the person is compliant. Old schoolers do not bend the rules; they use force and immediately give consequences for client misbehavior. Conflicted COs express concern about clients, yet have a negative perception of, and may feel threatened by them. These COs value protecting the public. Damaged COs experienced a negative incident on the job (e.g., client assault, lack of support from administration, etc.) resulting in their no longer wanting to support clients. Damaged COs are more likely to have an aggressive approach to clients and strictly enforce institutional rules for all violations. **King and Labrecque conclude that "it appears that better efforts are achieved when officers adopt a caring role."**[3]

According to the Merriam-Webster online dictionary, "**authoritarian**" is defined as: "of, relating to, or favoring blind submission to authority."[4] Dictionary.com defines authoritarian as: "favoring complete obedience or subjection to authority as opposed to individual freedom."[5] **Relationship-building** skills are a combination of techniques people use to communicate directly, create positive interactions, and build trusting alliances. I define a **therapeutic alliance** as an established working relationship between two people built on mutual respect, consideration, trust, dependability, honesty, listening, and assertiveness. These alliances are used by psychotherapists to help clients trust their counselor, identify their issues, verbalize thoughts and emotions, and learn/implement prosocial behaviors.

As mentioned earlier, I have worked with Colorado criminal halfway house administrators, case managers, and line staff; federal probation officers; and state parole and probation officers. I have also attended parole hearings administered by state parole board members. I have observed that these professionals fall into either the authoritarian or relationship-builder typology of their specific profession (see Chapter 2). Sometimes people will classify these criminal justice professional types simply as either authoritarian or social worker. I prefer to use the term relationship-builder rather than social worker because it lends itself to the establishment of a therapeutic alliance between justice system professional and client. I have observed that a continuum exists between the extreme authoritarian and relationship-builder COs, as evidenced by the research on typologies cited in the book American Prisons and Jails: An Encyclopedia of Controversies and Trends *by King and Labrecque, and my personal experiences. After working with justice system professionals for over forty years, I have concluded that they appear to favor either authoritarian or relationship-building philosophies, even if it is by a small amount.* ***Based on King and Labrecque's research and my experience, better rehabilitation results seem to occur when criminal justice professionals adopt relationship-building skills to interact with clients.***

How come? Although I will examine this issue in greater detail in subsequent chapters, I believe that human beings, no matter who they are, do not like to be told what to do unless they are specifically asking for advice. The United States' criminal justice system seems to dominate clients by aggressively telling them what to do throughout their entire justice system experience, sometimes beyond the regulations that an individual needs to adhere to, and whether they seek advice or not. When human beings are aggressively instructed to do something when not seeking advice, they tend to feel angry, depressed, and anxious, and may choose to be noncompliant. In general, research has shown that psychotherapists developing a therapeutic alliance with clients, more commonly called a healthy professional relationship, is psychologically healing. It can be deduced from this research that justice system professionals developing healthy, therapeutic relationships with those under correctional supervision will most likely improve their rehabilitation.

Psychological Reactance

Psychological Reactance Theory is a model that was proposed by American psychologist Jack W. Brehm in 1966. The American Psychological Association (APA) Dictionary of Psychology defines reactance theory as a model that suggests a person can experience this state as a response to a perceived threat or actual loss of a behavioral freedom. Reactance is a motivated state that causes discomfort, anxiety, and resistance, energizing a person to attempt to reduce and/or recover their lost freedom. When people are forced to give up a desired action, they often respond by pursuing the behavior that is lost. Often this results in a person doing the opposite of what they have been asked to do.[6] In the justice system world, this is usually labeled as client noncompliance.

For example, most people understand that scientific evidence suggests consuming too much sugar is unhealthy. When a person is told by their medical doctor to decrease their daily sugar intake, they often experience resistance because they don't want to lose their freedom to eat as many sweets as they would like. This may result in a patient's weight gain and/or other negative health consequences. People who employ psychological motivational interviewing (MI) techniques know this to be true and pursue changes by asking clients how the behavior in question is affecting them, rather than telling people what to do. A person using MI will ask a client what they believe their options are, and then a problem-solving discussion can occur. In this manner, the client has a say in how she/he will choose to address the issue.

A psychotherapist using MI techniques may ask a client who smokes cigarettes how this behavior is affecting their running exercise. Instead of suggesting to their client to stop smoking cigarettes (current evidence-based, common knowledge), which may be met with psychological reactance from the individual, the psychotherapist might ask the runner how smoking is affecting her/his overall performance. If the client states that their cigarette smoking is negatively affecting their running, the psychotherapist can inquire what behavioral options the runner is considering in order to problem-solve their smoking issue and improve their running performance. In this manner, the runner is deciding what they want to do rather than being told what to do (stop smoking), which could be met with psychological reactance, a strong resistance to giving up a behavioral freedom (smoking cigarettes).

Also, consequences of actions are often strong motivators to help people change their challenging behaviors. Burning one's hand on a hot stove will cause a person to be more cautious when using the stove. Evidence-based research supporting reactance theory has been produced by Sharon S. Brehm in 1981,[7] Paul J. Silvia in 2005,[8] and Claude H. Miller et al. in 2006.[9]

In the summer of 2003, Eric A. Seemann completed his psychology dissertation at Louisiana Tech University, titled "Personality Style and Psychological Reactance: Theory Confirmation and Empirical Prediction of Reactant Personalities." In his dissertation, Seemann cited research indicating psychological reactance is more of a characteristic of the person rather than the situation. Seemann's research examined ten hypotheses associated with personality types and psychological reactance. Although Seemann's sample size was relatively small, his research appears to be significant. Seemann's most important finding, for the purposes of this book, is that clients with high degrees of psychological reactance demonstrated higher levels of noncooperative, passive-aggressive, and aggressive character styles similar to antisocial personality disorder (ASPD) characteristics.

Most of the individuals that I facilitated counseling for in halfway houses exhibited ASPD characteristics. In the 2010 research study "Antisocial personality disorder in incarcerated offenders: Psychiatric comorbidity and quality of life," researchers Donald W. Black, Tracy Gunter, Peggy Loveless, Jeff Allen, and Bruce Sieleni found that 35.3 percent of newly incarcerated individuals were diagnosed with ASPD.[10] Many people involved in the US justice system appear to either have ASPD or, at the very least, some ASPD characteristics, and thus are probably more likely to exhibit higher levels of psychological reactance. Seeman further stated that individuals high in psychological reactance strongly value their personal freedom and control and will act out if they believe their behaviors are overly restricted.[11] It can be argued that an authoritarian, militaristic correctional environment, housing a majority of clients who exhibit ASPD characteristics, and most likely a high level of psychological reactance, is a set-up for antisocial-related behavior to occur. This idea is supported by the many correctional facility client demonstrations (sometimes called riots) that occur each year.

Psychological reactance provides us with another possible explanation as to why the United States' criminal justice system may incarcerate people for over-extended periods of time. Elongated prison sentences are a separate, important prison reform issue. Psychological reactance seems to play a significant role in client noncompliance and sentence extensions. Also, reactance seems to be involved in probation/parole violations, often causing a client's return to incarceration. Those under criminal justice supervision struggle when their case managers, COs, and parole and probation officers are overly aggressive and tell them what to do in an excessively authoritarian manner. Often the result is the client engaging in a noncompliant probation/parole-related behavior (e.g., using marijuana, drinking alcohol, violating curfew, not meeting justice system associated financial requirements, etc.), which can extend a client's sentence.

In contrast, being instructed what to do in an assertive, empathic, respectful manner, which takes into account the client's thoughts, feelings, and behaviors appears to be a better way for correction, probation and parole officers and line staff to attempt to have clients be compliant. *When I had to inform noncompliant halfway house clients of their need to attend additional counseling classes due to their alcohol/drug use, excessive anger incidents, violation of halfway house rules, and/or other problematic behaviors, I observed the client was more accepting of the consequence if I did so in a respectful and empathic manner. I also consider this approach to be professional and ethical. In my personal experience when someone who is incarcerated in a community corrections halfway house is told what to do in an assertive, respectful manner, they usually do what they were instructed to. I witnessed halfway house line staff (similar to COs) instruct clients: "Go to your room please."; "Please clean the staff room."; "Please clean your room."; "Please clean the bathrooms."; and observed clients being mostly compliant. When clients were given sanctions that they believed were overly aggressive and excessive, in a disrespectful, inappropriate, and/or unjustified manner ("Go to your room and do not leave until a line staff tells you to!" or "Do as I told you to do because I said so!"), they appeared to respond indirectly, outside the presence of their correctional supervisor, with noncompliance, possibly causing consequences that delayed the completion of their criminal sentence. This appears to be a psychological reactance response by a client. The client is told what to do in an aggressive, authoritarian manner, and she/he becomes angry, anxious, uncomfortable, and resistant in the face of possibly losing respect, independence, leisure time and/or any incarceration behavioral freedom. Ultimately, the client ends up doing the opposite of what was requested causing consequences that may result in a delay of her/his criminal sentence completion.*

To summarize, it has been my observation that people who work in the criminal justice field seem to generally fall into one of two categories. "**Authoritarians**" believe that people in the justice system need to be punished for their antisocial behavior and kept away from society until their debt has been paid. In contrast, "**relationship-builders**" believe that people who are incarcerated, on probation or parole need to receive psychological treatment and learn cognitive behavioral skills like assertiveness, anger management, parenting, alcohol/drug relapse prevention, decision-making, and rational thinking, in order to help them develop a prosocial lifestyle. Many relationship builders also believe that clients can benefit from psychologically processing their past traumatic experiences (i.e., ACEs; see Chapter 1, "Adverse Childhood Experiences [ACEs]"), which can be done in individual and/or group counseling sessions. At times, I have also encountered criminal justice professionals who are a combination of the authoritarian and relationship-builder, usually favoring one or the other typology.

Research and my experience suggest that it is important for justice system staff to exhibit a caring, assertive, empathic, relationship-building approach and be aware of psychological reactance in order to support client rehabilitation.

The Transtheoretical Model (TTM)—The Stages of Change

One of the definitions of rehabilitation found in the Merriam-Webster online dictionary is "the process of restoring someone (such as a criminal) to a useful and constructive place in society."[12]

Rehabilitation associated with the justice system has at times been more prominent, and at other times submerged. More recently it has experienced somewhat of a resurrection. Politics, violence, discrimination, police brutality, evidence-based research, prejudice, the prison reform movement, and the effects of crime on society have all influenced the justice system's approach to rehabilitation efforts. At the end of the 1970s, educational and vocational prison rehabilitation projects seemed to flourish. In the early 1980s, cognitive-behavioral alcohol/drug and domestic violence counseling also became commonly used methods of treatment for Americans driving under the influence of alcohol/drugs and experiencing anger management issues. The United States' war on drugs and focus on violent crime were prominent from the early to mid-1980s through the late 1990s, and the word rehabilitation in the justice system became almost nonexistent, replaced by punishment through elongated sentences. Over the past ten years, there has been some renewed vigor by people from all socioeconomic, gender, religious, racial, and professional backgrounds in support of prison reform and the need to therapeutically address the wide variety of correctional issues, giving new energy to rehabilitation efforts.

The Transtheoretical Model (TTM), also known as **The Stages of Change**, explains the process of how individuals can transform their behavior, including how those involved in the justice system can achieve rehabilitation. If a person is involved in the US justice system, it is usually due to allegedly breaking one of society's laws. Breaking society's laws is usually defined by the majority of the US public as an antisocial behavior. Rehabilitating the lawbreaker usually means helping them change their past antisocial actions to current prosocial (morally correct) behaviors.

The Stages of Change model was developed through behavioral research by James Prochaska and Carlo DiClemente in 1977. Changing unhealthy to healthy behaviors is challenging for most people. Many individuals who have tried to stop smoking cigarettes, maintain a better diet, and/or decrease or cease alcohol/drug use can attest to this statement. It is also true for those involved in the justice system who are attempting to change antisocial behaviors to prosocial ones. Prochaska and DiClemente discovered that transforming a behavior requires the individual to identify the issue, decide to alter the conduct, establish a plan, take action, and maintain the change.[13]

In my experience counseling people involved in the justice system, The Stages of Change model has provided an extremely valuable and rational approach to aiding clients. I was fortunate to attend a seminar in Denver, Colorado, in the early 1990s taught by the late Alan Marlatt, PhD, considered to be the father of alcohol/drug relapse prevention, and Carlo DiClemente, PhD. Marlatt and DiClemente spoke about substance use disorder, the stages individuals go through to make the change from using alcohol/drugs to abstinence, and how to maintain sobriety and prevent relapse. This process is very relevant for those involved in the justice system because the majority of clients have substance use disorder characteristics and can benefit from changing their alcohol/drug and antisocial actions to socially responsible consumption/sobriety and behaviors. **The key for transformation is that the individual has to want to change, be ready, and commit to it.**

The first stage of behavioral change is called **Precontemplation**. This stage does not involve change and is more about an individual's defending their current behavior, which they do not consider to be problematic, even when other people do. Precontemplation is similar to a denial defense mechanism in which the individual doesn't want to discuss the problematic behavior and/

or refutes that there is an issue. When a client is in the Precontemplation stage, I often ask them to attempt to be **mindful** (conscious) of the possibly problematic behavior and record how often the action occurs during each day for one week.

The second stage of change is **Contemplation**. In the Contemplation (or thinking) stage, individuals begin to make a list of all of the positive and negative attributes of their behavior in question (see Chapter 6, "3. Decision-Making"). Clients think about their problematic behavior and assign a score of 1-10 to the positive and negative attributes listed, based on how important each one is. The more important the item, the higher the score. Adding up the assigned points of the positive and negative items, the side with the highest score indicates the individual's preference using this decision-making technique. Even though the client is recognizing the negative aspects of the behavior in question, they still may not be ready to make a change. When the individual is ready to commit to changing the behavior and stopping or replacing it with a healthier alternative, they have completed the Contemplation stage and are ready to progress in the process of change.

The third stage of change is named **Preparation/Determination**. In the Preparation stage, clients committed to making a change create a written plan to either stop or change the problematic behavior and replace it with a healthy alternative. The individual commits to put their plan into action in one month, if not sooner. A cigarette smoker who has committed to stop smoking may decide to either use a harm reduction (gradual decrease over time which may result in abstinence) or a cold turkey (total abstinence at a designated time) plan. They may also plan to see their medical doctor to have their lungs evaluated and/or call their local quit smoking line for support. This plan may also include the individual informing family, friends, and acquaintances that they will quit smoking cigarettes on a specific date. Finally, the cigarette smoker may plan to attend a nicotine abstinence support group. Failing to make a plan can cause the process of change to be more haphazard and difficult to achieve. A written plan gives clients a concrete blueprint that supports them in implementing healthy change.

The fourth stage of change is **Action**. In this stage, people put their plan into motion. The individual has modified, stopped, or changed the behavior in question and possibly replaced it with a healthier option. The cigarette smoker has either decreased their intake or stopped smoking, had an appointment with their medical doctor, contacted a quit hotline, and informed family and friends that they are abstaining from nicotine. The cigarette smoker may also be attending a weekly nicotine abstinence support group. The individual may often remind themselves of their commitment to behavior change and develop a relapse prevention plan if applicable (see Chapter 6, "6. Alcohol/Drug Relapse [Recurrence] Prevention"). The client is implementing their behavior change plan, which may increase their therapeutic **self-efficacy: the belief they can successfully achieve their goal.**

The fifth stage of change is **Maintenance**. In this stage, the individual has changed or modified the challenging behavior and endured their transformation for at least six months and a day. Clients in this stage consciously guard against a relapse, the process of breaking their commitment to change their behavior. People in maintenance anticipate high-risk relapse situations (a predicament that increases the probability of returning to the problematic behavior) and develop coping skills to maintain their change. The cigarette smoker in maintenance has not used nicotine for more than six months, may avoid others who smoke, chew, and/or vape, and may continue to attend an abstinence support group. People who are making therapeutic changes can be hard on themselves when they experience natural urges and/or cravings to return to their past unhealthy behavior. Urges and cravings, the possible crux of substance use disorder, are very common experiences for individuals who have problematic alcohol/drug use characteristics and usually decrease over time with continued abstinence. Clients in the maintenance stage can benefit from their written relapse prevention plan, support from others, and recognition that urges and cravings are natural and change is difficult.

The sixth stage of change is **Termination**. In this stage, individuals have fully overcome their desire to engage in their problematic behavior. Clients are certain they will never relapse and report not experiencing urges and/or cravings for the problematic behavior. The cigarette smoker in the Termination stage has no urges or cravings to smoke and is certain, under all circumstances, that they will not use nicotine. Due to the possible genetic and environmental components of a substance use disorder, and the many complexities of ASPD, it appears that clients rarely reach the Termination stage. Alcoholics Anonymous (AA) seems to agree with this premise and supports group members continuing to attend meetings for as long as they feel the need to in order to remain sober. This may mean the individual will attend AA or another anonymous support group for the rest of their lives. Most justice professionals I have worked with agree with this, and it appears that clients who have progressed to the stable Maintenance stage remain in it as long as they do not relapse. The Termination stage of change seems to be infrequently achieved and too complex to verify, and therefore not always mentioned in the justice or health fields. A client's awareness of their problematic behavior, even in remission, seems to be helpful in maintaining their success.

TTM proposes that in order to be successful in stopping or transforming an unhealthy action to a healthy behavior, an individual needs to engage in **change processes. Change processes are thoughts, feelings, and behaviors that clients experience as they attempt to find solutions for their problematic behaviors. These processes can help individuals produce problem-solving techniques to stop unhealthy actions and establish and maintain healthy behaviors.**

TTM proposes that there are ten essential change processes, which are listed below:

1. **Consciousness Raising**: The individual gains a consciousness and understanding of the problematic action and increases their awareness of healthy behavior alternatives.
2. **Dramatic Relief**: The client becomes conscious of, and expresses the emotions associated with the problem behavior and possible solutions.
3. **Environmental Reevaluation**: The person realizes how their problematic behavior affects other people.
4. **Self-Reevaluation**: The client uses cognitive reframing, changing the way they think (about the problematic behavior), to include exhibiting healthy behaviors. The nicotine user, who thinks he portrays himself as hip when vaping, may decide to quit, due to his health becoming more important than his perceived appearance in public.
5. **Self-Liberation**: The individual chooses to make a commitment to change the problematic behavior and believes they have the ability to do so successfully (self-efficacy).
6. **Counterconditioning**: The person replaces the problem behavior with a healthy alternative. For example, meditative breathing (deep, slow, in and out breathing) can replace smoking a cigarette.
7. **Helping Relationships**: The individual accepts other people's support to help them change their problematic behavior. Support groups like AA can be a part of helping relationships.
8. **Social Liberation**: The person becomes conscious of their environment supporting their healthy behavior change attempt.

9. **Stimulus Control**: The individual recognizes what they can and can't control in their environment, their need to avoid problem behavior triggers, and the necessity to engage in healthy actions instead.
10. **Reinforcement Management**: The person finds ways to reward the positive behavior and decrease the benefits of the negative action.

TTM has been shown to have limitations that are important to be aware of. The following are some of these limitations. TTM does not take into account how ready someone is to change, and how an individual's income might affect their progress through the stages. The model also does not provide a set of valid criteria indicating a person's actual stage of change. TTM does not give an estimate as to how much time is needed for someone to complete a stage of change and the entire transformation process. The Stages of Change model also seems to assume that clients use rational thinking to make decisions; however, this may not be the case.[14] Finally, antisocial personality and substance use disorder-related behaviors, which those involved in the justice system often exhibit, appear to be caused by environmental and genetic factors. TTM focuses on behavioral change, which may not address a client's genetic factors.

If justice system workers choose to take on, as one of their professional responsibilities, the act of restoring those under correctional supervision to a constructive place in their community, this will benefit themselves and clients. By understanding TTM, justice system workers have another opportunity to help achieve one of their corrections goals, which is to provide treatment support for clients (see Chapter 2, "Corrections"). This can benefit client rehabilitation efforts by possibly decreasing recidivism.

For many people, change is difficult. We get comfortable with our behavior patterns, no matter how unhealthy they may be. Change requires a tremendous amount of determination, which includes awareness, desire, commitment, planning, motivation, action, and maintenance. People involved in the justice system are asked to change their problematic, antisocial actions into morally responsible, prosocial behaviors and lifestyles.

Understanding how people change, their readiness to transform, and the obstacles that may exist in this process will aid justice system workers in helping clients develop a prosocial lifestyle. A correctional worker sharing their knowledge of TTM can help a willing client recognize, understand, and process their ambivalence to change. TTM benefits justice system professionals by helping them understand the process of change that individuals go through, which in turn may increase COs' empathy, client success rates, and workers' employment satisfaction. Clients benefit from TTM by understanding that change is actually a process, takes time and determination, and is difficult. TTM can help clients change antisocial to prosocial behaviors and justice system workers accomplish their professional responsibility of client rehabilitation.

Conclusion

Understanding clients' and justice system professionals' personality characteristics, psychological reactance, and The Stages of Change can help improve rehabilitation success rates and correctional workers' job satisfaction. Gaining knowledge about CO typologies and the character of those involved in the justice system allows these two groups the possibility of better understanding each other and working together to improve employment satisfaction and rehabilitation.

Psychological reactance gives us another possible way to understand how come those involved in the justice system respond so strongly when they perceive a behavioral freedom has been taken away. A justice system worker who understands psychological reactance may be able to respond to a client in a more empathic and calm manner and possibly deescalate a potentially dangerous situation. Through the use of role-modeling, this response may teach a client how to better control their emotions (**emotional regulation**), calm themselves, and utilize rational thinking to problem-solve.

Understanding the evidence-based Stages of Change model benefits both those under correctional supervision and justice system workers. Motivated clients pursuing a prosocial lifestyle may be able to embrace the process involved in TTM and accept that change takes time. This may also allow clients to be more self-accepting and less hard on themselves. Justice system workers can utilize TTM to attempt to identify the stage of change a client is in, discuss it with an inquiring individual, suggest problem-solving techniques if asked, and have increased empathy for this person. This can be very helpful to a client, support rehabilitation, and improve a justice system worker's esteem. Understanding the Precontemplation, Contemplation, Preparation, Action, and Maintenance Stages of Change can also help clients be more patient with the process, and justice system workers recognize the person under correctional supervision is considering positive alternatives. The ten change processes associated with TTM can be added to a client's and a justice system worker's therapeutic tool bag. The change processes are therapeutic, rational, problem-solving techniques that can be easily taught and implemented.

Understanding CO typologies, clients' character traits, psychological reactance, and The Stages of Change can help improve general rehabilitation efforts and justice system workers' employment success and satisfaction.

teach a client how to better control their emotions (emotional regulation), calm themselves, and utilize rational thinking correctly [illegible].

Understanding the evidence-based Stages of Change model benefits both those under correctional supervision and justice system workers. [illegible] Clients attending a [illegible] [illegible]

[illegible]

4

Justice System Personnel, Their Qualifications, and the Mental Health Training They Receive

Every interaction that a justice system staff member has with a person involved in the justice system is an opportunity to add to the client's rehabilitative progress. Justice system professionals working together to implement therapeutic techniques have an opportunity to have a cumulative positive effect on clients, potentially resulting in expedited rehabilitation and decreased recidivism.

The purpose of this chapter is to identify and understand the qualifications of the wide range of criminal justice professionals who interact with clients, and the mental health training that they receive. This chapter summarizes these justice system workers' basic employment descriptions and the client mental health instruction they generally receive. The benefits of training justice system personnel in mental health and interpersonal skills will also be discussed.

This chapter is not intended to be an in-depth description of all of the professions involved in the criminal justice system. Many correctional employment resources offer in-depth work descriptions available to the interested reader.

The next section of this chapter is an attempt to acknowledge the many criminal justice employment opportunities that exist in the police, corrections, and court systems. Please feel free to read these entire sections for a complete understanding of justice system employment opportunities, the minimum qualifications of each vocation, and the mental health training they receive, or skip to your particular area of interest.

Justice System Personnel Employment Descriptions

People who work in federal, state, or local prisons, jails, halfway houses, work release programs, and courts, as well as police, peace, public safety, parole, probation, and pretrial officers can have a profound effect on those involved in the justice system. These professions are organized below into corrections, the police, and courts separately.

1. Corrections

In the US correctional system, wardens, also known as superintendents, directors, or administrators, are usually the people responsible for running a prison/jail operation and may have an executive assistant for support.[1] Wardens and their assistants ensure that the correctional facility meets safety standards for all their personnel and those involved in the justice system. Wardens are responsible for managing the correctional facility's finances and the performance of all staff members. A facilities manager often oversees staff, makes sure that clients are receiving appropriate care, and generally is in charge of the daily functioning of the correctional institution.

Correctional and detention officers, and security guards and technicians, are generally responsible for enforcing facility rules, supervising clients, searching for contraband, resolving client and client–CO disputes, inspecting the institution, and helping with the rehabilitation of those involved in the justice system.

Correctional case managers, unit office managers, and librarians assist with a client's transition to incarceration. Correctional case managers evaluate a person's psychological treatment needs and produce and monitor program plans designed to help rehabilitate clients. Case managers may also support a client's reintegration into society. The unit office manager answers clients' general questions and provides clerical and administrative support to the correctional staff. Librarian duties include managing all library services and procedures, assisting clients' and staff's library needs, cataloging materials, and monitoring patrons.

Physicians, dentists, nurses, and emergency medical technicians (EMTs) provide a wide variety of medical care for those incarcerated in the justice system. They provide basic medical care, emergency services, medication administration, and limited mental health services. Dentists provide basic dental care for those involved in the justice system.

Psychologists, social workers, as well as professional and substance abuse and group counselors, and rehabilitation and behavioral specialists provide psychological, mental health, and substance use disorder counseling services for clients. Prison chaplains provide spiritual services and counseling for those who are incarcerated and justice system staff.

Recreation and activities specialists coordinate and facilitate correctional facility leisure activities. These activities may include exercise, sports, movies, board games, meditation, arts and crafts, and music.

Maintenance workers repair and maintain the correctional facilities. Maintenance workers may supervise people involved in the justice system.

Food service workers prepare and serve food in the correctional facility as well as engage in food-related clean-up activities. Food service workers may supervise clients in all of these actions.[2]

2. Community Corrections

Community corrections, also known as "comcor," usually refers to those incarcerated in halfway houses or work release programs, or on probation or parole. Community corrections incarceration may be staffed by some of the already stated corrections personnel, including directors, administrators, case managers, individual and group substance use and mental health counselors, maintenance, and food service workers. Line staff observe the daily activities of clients who are incarcerated in community corrections halfway houses. They enforce facility rules and monitor the general environment of the halfway house and the clients' whereabouts in the community.

Vocational specialists and counselors help clients prepare for and find employment opportunities. They can help clients understand their career options, improve their job-seeking skills, and may provide employment training. Vocational counselors employed in US federal prisons and jails usually assist clients by training them in trade and work-related skills needed to gain employment.

Probation and parole officers supervise clients who live in the community to ensure they are abiding by designated rules and regulations. They support those involved in the justice system in order to help them readapt to general society. Probation can be a legal ruling given to a client as an alternative to jail or prison. Probation is often used for nonviolent and lower-risk clients convicted of misdemeanors or minor felonies. Probation officers usually work with clients who have been sentenced to community corrections (halfway house, work release, and probation) rather than prison. Oftentimes, someone on probation has had their prison sentence suspended. Also, a compliant, successful client who is in prison or jail can be granted probation and released to the community before their sentence is completed to help them reintegrate into society. A probation officer can regress noncompliant clients on probation back to court, which may result in the person receiving a more severe legal sentence.

Parole is the early release of a usually compliant client from incarceration in a prison to community supervision. Parole is usually a client's conditional release from prison granted by a state parole board or the federal United States Parole Commission (USPC). Paroled individuals are usually higher risk clients. The client can live in the community while they are in the process of completing their sentence. Clients on parole who do not abide by the designated rules can be regressed back to incarceration (see Chapter 2, "Corrections").

Pretrial officers provide community supervision to people involved in the justice system who are released from incarceration after their arrest and before their court trial begins. Pretrial officers usually assess the level of community supervision their client needs.[3]

3. The Police

As stated in Chapter 2, in the section "The Police," the responsibility of the police and peace officers in the United States is to maintain a safe environment for people in the community. Police and peace officers' duties include identifying and preventing all types of crime and enforcing the established laws of society. Police and peace officers address crime, promote public safety by maintaining an atmosphere of peace and security in neighborhoods, and provide many types of emergency services. Police control crime by upholding the rule of law, investigating unlawful acts, and arresting alleged suspects. They maintain public safety by attempting to control large assemblies of people, family disputes (which may include domestic violence), and vehicle congestion. People usually call the police when any kind of emergency occurs in a neighborhood and when they are unsure of who else to contact.

There are many different types of vocations in police and peace officer work including detectives, investigators, state troopers, sheriffs, FBI agents, Border Patrol, security guards, transit, narcotics, code enforcement, customs, school resource, public safety, university/campus, U.S. Immigration and Customs Enforcement (ICE), park rangers, and air or sky marshals. For the purposes of this book, the discussion will include police and peace officers who are in contact with people who are, or are about to be, involved with the justice system.

4. The Court System

In the United States, criminal court system judges, lawyers, paralegals, bailiffs, and court interpreters usually have the most interactions with those involved in the justice system. The judge supervises the court process, ensures proceedings are legally correct, instructs juries, and sentences clients. The judge is responsible for ensuring that a client receives a legal and fair trial.

There are two types of lawyers in criminal courts: the prosecuting and the defense attorneys. The prosecutor, also known as the district attorney (DA), represents the government and pursues truth and justice when a person is accused of committing a crime. The defense attorney acts on behalf of the accused person, also called a defendant. The defense attorney basically protects the legal rights of the accused individual. A client may hire and pay for a defense attorney. If a person is unable to afford a private defense attorney, the court may appoint a public defender for the client. A public defender is a defense attorney who is usually an employee of the government. Attorneys may have paralegals, also known as legal assistants, to help with their caseload.

The bailiff is the courtroom official who provides security and safety for all courtroom participants. The bailiff also maintains general order and keeps control of the courtroom.

The court interpreter translates information from another language to English, and vice versa for judges, lawyers, defendants, witnesses, and court staff.[4]

The Minimum Employment Qualifications for Justice System Personnel

To discuss the minimum employment qualifications justice system professionals need to obtain, I will again group these into corrections, the police and the courts. The purpose of this section is to provide a general idea of the education, training, and instruction justice system workers receive. Again, this is not meant to be a comprehensive description of the education received by justice system staff. Also, it is essential to keep in mind that each state and the federal government usually have different specific minimum qualifications and training requirements for all correctional employment positions.

The minimum requirements for correctional, police and court employment in the United States usually include being at least twenty-one years of age and a US citizen, obtaining a high school diploma or General Educational Development (GED) diploma/certificate, having no felony convictions, eligibility to own/possess a firearm, being physically healthy and fit, submitting a negative drug screen, passing a background check, and possessing good relational skills.

1. Corrections

Wardens, superintendents, prison directors, administrators, and facility managers are some of the highest level correctional employment positions in the US criminal justice system. The requirements to become an administrative justice system professional are usually having a Bachelor of Arts (BA) college degree in business, public administration, criminal justice, social work, psychology, criminology, or behavioral science, and five years of experience working in corrections. An administrative justice system professional may have earned a Master of Arts (MA) degree. Many people who become correctional wardens and administrators begin their criminal justice careers as corrections officers and progress through promotions.

Correctional officer (CO), security guard, technician, and detention agent employment requirements vary from state to state. The usual minimum requirements for these employment opportunities are stated in the second paragraph of this section ("The Minimum Employment Qualifications for Justice System Personnel") with the addition of prospective COs needing to attend a CO training academy for at least three weeks and sometimes as long as five or more months. Most federal CO requirements include having a BA degree or at least three years of employment experience in a medical, counseling, teaching, and/or supervising field.[5, 6]

Prospective COs are usually required to participate in an academy-like, intensive residential training program similar to that which police officer recruits usually attend. CO training is usually a combination of classroom-based instruction focusing on correctional, professional, ethical, and legal information, as well as defensive strategies to deal with violent clients and possible incarceration-related riots. CO training may include instruction on communication, de-escalation techniques, and self-defense. CO academy programs can also provide educational instruction on physical conditioning, firearms training, restraining techniques, facility searches, first aid, emergency procedures, and CPR. Finally, COs are responsible for supporting the rehabilitation efforts of those involved in the justice system. In general, correctional facilities have increased their client rehabilitation efforts by offering mental health, substance use, vocational and educational classes and programs. COs may be required to have a fundamental knowledge of these rehabilitative programs and recognize clients that are eligible and wanting to participate in them.[7]

Each state can impose their own correctional case manager requirements. A correctional case manager is usually required to have earned a minimum of an Associate of Arts college degree (AA, two years), and more likely a bachelor's degree (four to five years), and many even have a master's degree (one to two years after completing a BA degree) from an accredited college. Usually, a prospective correctional case manager's college major is criminal justice, sociology, criminology, psychology, counseling, social work, or behavioral science. Some states require correctional case managers to be certified or licensed, which may call for the individual to pass an employment-specific certification or licensing test. Most correctional case managers initially work as a trainee, assistant, or intern, and are usually required to observe and shadow a skilled case manager.[8]

The requirements to become a correctional unit office manager may include four years of post-high school education or one to three years of specialized relevant work experience in clerical, office, and/or administrative support.[9]

The requirements to become a correctional librarian may include having a bachelor's degree in library science or a related field of study from an accredited college and two years of work experience in a library. A master's or doctorate degree in library science or a related field may be substituted for professional experience.[10]

A correctional physician's minimum qualification is usually a license to practice medicine as a medical doctor or doctor of osteopathy in the state they work in. In order to receive a medical doctor license in the United States, an applicant needs to obtain an undergraduate college degree, graduate from medical school (four years), and complete a residency program, or specialized training, usually lasting at least three years. The correctional physician usually must be board eligible or certified by the appropriate board recognized by the American Medical Association (AMA) in either Family, Emergency, Internal, Physical and/or Preventive Medicine.[11] A correctional psychiatrist has similar minimum qualifications as a correctional physician along with a four-year residency, three of which are in psychiatric care.

The minimum qualifications to become a correctional nurse in the United States are that the applicant must have an associate (practical nurse, LPN) or bachelor's (registered nurse, RN) degree in nursing and pass the applicable NCLEX-PN (practical nurse) or the NCLEX-RN (registered nurse) exam. The NCLEX-PN-RN exams are the national nursing tests that a person must pass in order to be licensed before practicing nursing. Nurses must be licensed in the state where they plan to work before starting employment. In addition to the national exams, each state has its own requirements for nurses.[12]

The minimum qualifications to become a correctional EMT are usually obtaining a high school diploma or GED, cardiopulmonary resuscitation (CPR) certification, and licensing from the state in which the EMT plans to be employed. On average, aspiring EMTs attend training programs that last from four months to two years. EMT training programs usually include evaluating patients' health conditions and dealing with emergency and trauma situations. The NREMT AEMT Exam is a national test that aspiring EMTs may need to pass to receive licensing. Although the NREMT AEMT exam is recognized in most states, a person needs to meet the specific EMT licensing requirements of the state they plan to work in.[13]

The minimum qualifications for a correctional dentist are usually that the applicant has obtained a college undergraduate degree, passed the Dental Admissions Test (DAT), graduated from a four-year dental school, and received a Doctor of Dental Medicine (DMD) or Doctor of Dental Surgery (DDS) degree from an American Dental Association (ADA) approved school. A correctional dentist may have completed a one-to three-year residency program and needs to have a current, valid dentist license issued by the state dental board in which the dentist plans to practice, and two years of licensed dentist experience.[14]

Correctional psychologists, clinical social workers, professional counselors, substance abuse, mental health, group and rehabilitation counselors, and behavioral specialists provide mental health treatment and services for those involved in the justice system. These services include assessment, diagnosis, testing, treatment planning, and facilitating individual and/or group substance use, mental health, and rational thinking counseling for those involved in the justice system.

Correctional psychologists are usually required to have completed a doctoral degree, finished a psychological internship, and be licensed by the state in which they are employed. Correctional licensed clinical social workers and professional counselors usually need to earn a bachelor's and a master's degree, complete an internship, and be licensed by the state in which they work. Substance use, rehabilitation, mental health and group counselors, and behavioral specialists usually are required to possess at least a bachelor's degree, and many have a master's degree. Depending on a specific state's requirements, these positions may require passing specialized tests and/or obtaining a national or state license or certification.

Correctional recreation and activities specialists are usually required to have a bachelor's degree with a major study in recreation or three years of work experience in recreation, or a combination of education and practical experience.[15] Prison chaplains are usually required to have obtained at least a bachelor's degree in pastoral counseling. Many states and the federal government call for the applicant to possess a Master of Divinity (MDiv) degree from an American Theological School, with twenty graduate study hours of 1) theology; 2) ministry courses; 3) sacred writings; and 4) comparative religions or church history. Prison chaplains are also frequently required to have two years of experience working in a ministry setting.[16]

Correctional maintenance staff include, yet are not limited to, automotive mechanics, carpenters, custodians, electricians, HVAC (heating, ventilation and air conditioning) workers, painters, plumbers, and upholsterers.

Correctional maintenance staff are usually required to have obtained a high school diploma or GED and have knowledge and skills associated with their specific technical practices, necessary equipment, tools, and materials to perform their employment responsibilities. Most maintenance staff may build, maintain, and/or repair items in their specific area of expertise. Specific maintenance staff may need to have passed professional tests and/or obtained certifications and/or licenses and have work-related experience. Also, correctional maintenance staff are often required to supervise those involved in the justice system.[17]

Correctional food service workers are usually required to have the skill of being successful at quantity cooking and supervising others, acquired through meal preparation experience and/or training. Food service staff usually supervise those involved in the justice system in cooking, meat cutting, baking, handling and storing food, and meal clean up.[18]

2. Community Corrections

Many community corrections employee qualifications, including directors, administrators, case managers, individual and group substance use, and mental health counselors, maintenance, and food service workers have already been discussed. Correctional line staff are usually required to be twenty-one years old, possess a high school diploma or GED, have no felony convictions, and sometimes have correctional work experience.[19]

Vocational specialists, also called employment, occupational, career, and rehabilitation counselors, are sometimes employed by community corrections and state prisons. Federal correctional institutions usually offer vocational training based on client and general society employment needs. Those involved in the federal justice system may receive on-the-job training administered by expert instructors via correctional facility employment assignments.[20] Correctional vocational counselors' minimum qualifications are usually a bachelor's degree and work experience. Many vocational counselors are required to have a master's degree. Depending on a specific state's requirements, vocational counselors may also be required to pass specialized tests and/or obtain a national or state license or certification.[21]

Federal and state parole officer minimum requirements usually include the applicant obtaining a bachelor's degree in criminal justice, sociology, psychology, corrections, or social work, and having a driver's license. Prospective parole officers usually need to finish a related internship, pass a psychological test, and complete required federal or state certifications, including one for firearms. Parole officers usually carry firearms. Parole officers are often required to attend an academy similar to that of an aspiring police officer or CO. Parole officers also usually need to complete on-the-job field training with a senior parole officer after hiring.[22]

Federal and state probation, and pretrial officer minimum educational requirements are similar to those of their parole officer counterparts, and they also need to possess a driver's license. Other probation and pretrial officer minimum requirements may include completing police academy-like and/or officer safety training. Probation and pretrial officers may also need to pass federal-or state-required tests and obtain specific certifications. Probation and pretrial officers may or may not carry firearms and/or need to complete firearms training, depending on state requirements. Probation and pretrial officer requirements vary from state to state.[23]

3. The Police

Police officers' basic minimum requirements are usually those listed in the second paragraph of this section ("The Minimum Employment Qualifications for Justice System Personnel"). Every state has a Commission on Peace Officer Standards (POST) or an equivalent board that creates minimum requirements for police officers. These requirements vary from state to state. Although most states call for police to have a high school diploma or GED, other states require the applicant to have some college coursework completion or a bachelor's degree. College subjects associated with police work include criminal justice, psychology, sociology, social work, and corrections.[24]

Police officers are usually required to attend and graduate from a police academy. A police academy, also known as field, recruit, and law enforcement training, instructs people on how to become officers of the law. Those attending the police academy receive classroom and physical training instruction that helps officers learn how to deal with the specific challenges of law enforcement work. Although police academies in the United States do not have a standardized curriculum, most law enforcement training is similar. The average time it takes to complete the academy is five months.

Most police officers are hired and then attend the academy soon afterwards. Police academy academic curriculum may include, yet is not limited to, legal knowledge, report writing, accident investigation, vehicle operation, safe driving, arrest procedures, incident reporting, firearms and weapons training, community relations, emergency treatment, first aid including CPR, civil rights, negotiation, communication, client psychology, courtroom testimony, risk assessment, resilience, use of force and perseverance.[25]

4. The Court System

Most federal and state criminal court judges have achieved notable educational and work experience accomplishments. The US Constitution doesn't list justice (judge) qualifications regarding citizenship, age, and profession for the Supreme Court.[26] Specific requirements to become a judge vary from state to state.

The usual minimum requirements to become a judge are to initially attend an accredited college, obtain a bachelor's degree, and take the Law School Admission Test (LSAT). After completing a Juris Doctor degree (JD) from an

American Bar Association (ABA) accredited law school, which can take three to four years, a prospective judge will need to pass the bar exam in the state that they desire to practice law and become a judge in. Once an individual passes the bar exam in their desired state, they are licensed to practice law in that state. Usually, substantial work experience as an attorney can help a lawyer ultimately become a judge. Prospective judges need to be appointed or elected. To obtain a judgeship appointment, a person must meet the minimum requirements to become a judge in their desired state, propose themselves to a nomination committee, and be selected to become a judge.[27]

The minimum qualifications to become a public defender, defense attorney, district attorney, or prosecuting attorney are the same as for a prospective judge, except there is no need for a lawyer who does not want to be a judge to seek a nomination to be appointed to become one. Related work experience in their desired area of law expertise usually helps attorneys professionally advance.

The minimum requirements to become a paralegal, also known as a legal assistant, are usually to complete an associate or bachelor's degree from an ABA-approved program and to comply with the rules of the state they want to work in. Some states may require that a legal assistant complete a paralegal certification.[28]

The minimum qualifications to become a bailiff are usually the same as the basic requirements to work in the US criminal justice system. These employment requirements are listed in the second paragraph of this section ("Minimum Employment Qualifications for Justice System Personnel"). In addition, experience working in the criminal justice system may be required.[29]

The usual minimum requirements to become a professional court interpreter are to have an excellent mastery of English and another language, at least two years of college experience, and interpretation skills.[30] Court interpreters are also usually required to complete an interpreter training program and pass certification exams.[31] Court interpreter qualifications vary from state to state.

Justice System Employee Mental Health Training

1. Basic Correctional and Police Officer Mental Health Training

People involved in the justice system experience a wide range of psychological challenges and substance use disorder characteristics, and often a combination of both. In an October 2023 blog post "Unlocking Wellness Behind the Bars: Illuminating the Struggles and Triumphs of Mental Health in Prisons," author Amanda Beltrani, PhD, a licensed forensic and clinical psychologist, writes that people incarcerated in prisons in the United States experience depression, post-traumatic stress disorder (PTSD), substance use disorders, bipolar disorder, personality disorders, schizophrenia, and other psychotic disorders, suicidal ideation, and self-harm at higher rates than the general public. Those incarcerated in US prisons also experience anxiety disorders at approximately the same rate as the general public. Beltrani goes on to write that "No universally accepted standard specifies a precise number of mental health professionals per inmate or a fixed number of therapy hours per month" (for clients experiencing psychological issues). Beltrani suggests that training of correctional staff in identifying and attending to clients' mental health issues can help improve their psychological challenges.[32]

In reviewing research associated with the mental health issues of those involved in the justice system and required training for corrections staff, police, and courtroom personnel, it appears that there is no mandatory, universal course of instruction. Correctional, police, probation, parole, and pretrial officers are usually required to attend an intensive, residential training academy. These academies offer correction-related classroom education, constructive defense skills, and usually some basic, limited client mental health training. According to the CorrectionalOfficerEdu.org website article, *Corrections Officer Training*, most COs attend "Rehabilitative Methods Training" at the academy. As explained by this article, federal and state correctional facilities have attempted to decrease client recidivism by increasing mental health, substance use, vocational and educational programs. COs are informed about these therapeutic programs and how to identify clients who may benefit from them.[33]

The National Commission on Correctional Health Care (NCCHC) is a nonprofit organization, originally established by the American Medical Association in 1983. The NCCHC's mission is to improve the standard of health care for all correctional facilities (prisons, jails, and juvenile corrections) in the United States. The NCCHC conducts "voluntary" correctional facility physical and mental health and opioid treatment accreditation programs. US correctional facilities are not required to be accredited by the NCCHC, yet their endorsement seems to be very beneficial. **The NCCHC produced Standards for Mental Health Services in Correctional Facilities, "MH-C-04 Mental Health Training for Correctional Officers," which requires that all COs who work with those involved in the justice system receive yearly mental health training.** This training includes learning to identify symptoms of mental illnesses, substance use, and cognitive issues. The suggested training instructs COs about how to communicate with those involved in the justice system who are experiencing these issues. The NCCHC also recommends COs learn suicide prevention and intervention techniques, and how to refer clients who are experiencing psychological distress to the appropriate mental health professionals. Finally, the NCCHC suggests COs assigned to mental health correctional facility areas receive additional sexual harassment and abuse training.[34]

2. Correctional and Police Officer Mental Health Training in Detail

Based on a review of the research, there appears to be a lack of mandatory, standardized training for all US police, peace, and COs that teaches the skills to help them therapeutically interact with clients experiencing mental health issues. Most police academies include course instruction similar to the "Rehabilitative Methods Training," discussed earlier, that many COs receive.

Police, peace, and COs may also likely attend "**Mental Health First Aid For Public Safety**," an eight-hour course that teaches them about mental health issues and substance use disorders. This course is designed to provide officers with professional behavior options to de-escalate challenging situations and maintain a safe environment. "Mental Health First Aid For Public Safety" is an evidence-based process that helps officers recognize the warning signs of mental health issues, intervene as early as possible, and engage in crisis intervention. **In addition, many police forces have implemented Crisis Intervention Teams (CITs) to therapeutically interact with people experiencing serious psychological challenges.** Police CIT members usually attend a forty-hour training that offers a specific curriculum designed to decrease the risk of injury when officers are interacting with people who are experiencing mental health issues. The CIT course helps officers better understand mental health issues and develop communication skills to aid those experiencing serious psychological challenges. The police attending a CIT course usually interact with mental health professionals during their training.[35]

Empathy training is usually considered to be an educational program designed to teach people how to understand, experience, and share the emotions and perspectives that other individuals are encountering, and to respond appropriately.[36] As will be discussed in detail in future chapters of this book, empathy can be considered to be a therapeutic healing component of justice system personnel-client relationships. Although empathy trainings are available in the US criminal justice system, it is difficult to find information about what percentage of workers actually receive this type of education.

Effective Practices in Community Supervision (EPICS) is an evidence-based training program designed to help probation and parole officers and other criminal justice employees implement client rehabilitative techniques using a structured approach. This method can incorporate the use of a client check-in, review, intervention, and homework assignment each meeting. EPICS techniques include role modeling, reinforcement, therapeutic disapproval of antisocial behavior, justice system worker–client collaboration, cognitive restructuring, skill building, and problem-solving. EPICS has been successful in reducing recidivism. Problematic EPICS issues include not all justice system employees receive this training, worker noncompliance, challenging client-justice system employee relationships, and training costs.[37]

Recent studies have provided evidence that police and CO trainings are beneficial to law enforcement, civilians, and possibly those involved in the justice system. The National Initiative for Building Community Trust and Justice was a United States Department of Justice program that existed from 2014 to 2019. It was designed to increase trust between communities and the criminal justice system using the "procedural justice" approach. **According to The National Institute for Building Community Trust and Justice, "procedural justice" is understood as the manner in which police and other authorities communicate with civilians, and how the characteristics of these interactions influence the public's opinions of the police, law abidance and crime rates.** Procedural justice police techniques are based on fairness and giving civilians the opportunity to be listened to and respected, while peace officers exhibit neutrality and trustworthiness. It is based on the police treating citizens fairly, being impartial and transparent in law enforcement decision-making, listening to civilians, and building trust with communities.[38] In a 2021 study titled "Reforming the Police Through Procedural Justice Training: A Multicity Randomized Trial at Crime Hot Spots," the researchers trained a total of twenty-eight police officers in procedural justice techniques in three US cities: Tucson, AZ; Cambridge, MA; and Houston, TX. **The researchers found that officers implementing procedural justice techniques resulted in increased fair behavior practices with civilians and crime prevention. This research confirmed that police employing procedural justice techniques**

can lead to a decrease in arrests by officers and crime, and an increase in civilians having a positive opinion of the police.[39]

The results of a 2021 national survey examining client mental health training taught in police academies and departments across the United States revealed that such instruction has significantly increased over the last twenty years. This survey indicated that most police departments reported using crisis intervention-like teams (CITs) to deal with mental health crisis calls. The survey also disclosed that law enforcement agencies believe their management of mental health-related situations is effective.[40]

CO trainings are beneficial to COs and most likely those involved in the justice system. In an analysis titled "Addressing the Mental Health Needs of Inmates Through Education for Correctional Officers—A Narrative Review," produced in 2023, the authors state that the number of people incarcerated in correctional facilities and diagnosed with a mental illness is disproportionately high. The authors conducted a review of mental health education programs offered to COs. The authors reported that educational trainings resulted in COs improving their information about, point of view toward, and therapeutic skills implemented with clients. This review went on to say that these improvements decreased after the training was completed. The review stated that COs were receptive to trainers that had correctional or mental health work experience. **Most importantly, the study's authors concluded that education programs offered to COs were beneficial.** Finally, the authors suggested that ongoing, consistent mental health education and training programs for COs may address the issue of COs retaining client mental health-related information for longer periods of time after trainings are completed.[41]

While at the present time there are no mandatory, universal mental health training courses offered for all US police, peace, correctional, probation, parole and/or pretrial officers, it appears that more of these professionals have engaged in this type of training than ever before. The academies and continuing educational courses offered to, and in some cases mandated by these professions, have apparently increased client mental health awareness in the criminal justice system. Increased mental health training and awareness may advance correctional rehabilitation efforts and decrease recidivism.

Correctional case managers, nurses, psychologists, social workers, substance use, rehabilitation, vocational and group counselors, behavioral specialists, prison chaplains, line staff, judges, lawyers, and paralegals usually have obtained, at a minimum, an associate degree, and many have a bachelor's, master's, or doctorate degree. Most have studied psychology, sociology, criminology, behavioral science, social work, or criminal justice. This knowledge seems to help these professionals better interact with clients who experience mental health issues. As indicated by the above studies, increased mental health awareness, education, and training may improve therapeutic interactions with clients. It also appears that criminal justice system personnel can benefit from receiving advanced training in empathy and client mental health issues. These therapeutic interactions, in turn, may improve client rehabilitation and justice system worker employment success and satisfaction and decrease recidivism.

A Note About Correctional and Police Officer Stressors

The significant employment stress experienced by correctional and police officers may be an important factor decreasing client rehabilitation efforts and possibly leading to current staff shortages in both professions. These staff shortages most likely have negative effects on correctional and police officers, as well as those involved in the justice system. Insufficient staffing can cause correctional and police officer overwork, physical and mental exhaustion, and personnel inconsistencies. Inadequate staffing may further decrease dependable law enforcement and rehabilitation efforts.

A Vera Institute of Justice article titled "The Prison Experience for Corrections Staff" states that people who work inside correctional facilities are responsible for the stressful job of maintaining a safe environment. This article reports that preliminary studies indicate corrections officers experience PTSD, depression, and death by suicide at much higher rates than law enforcement staff in other agencies, military personnel, and the general public. The article argues that low pay, limited emotional support, and understaffing create inadequate working conditions for COs. Finally, the article indicates that mundane routines, violence on the job, overtime demands, having to deal with crisis situations, possible risk of injury, lack of support from or trust in supervisors, and inadequate training can lead to serious physical and psychological issues.[42]

"Understanding Police Officer Stress: A Review of the Literature," researched by H. Douglas Otto and Alysson Gatens, and produced by the Illinois Criminal Justice Information Authority in 2022, is an analysis of information examining the effects of trauma and stress on the well-being of police officers. Otto's and Gatens' review indicates that law enforcement officers are often subjected to traumatic, violent, and very challenging situations that can cause serious stress. This review suggests that police officers can also experience stress associated with employment dissatisfaction and discrimination. The stress police encounter can result in physical, mental, and emotional exhaustion as well as PTSD, which officers experience at higher rates than that of the general public.[43]

Correctional and police officer employment stressors are significant and can result in their experiencing serious physical and psychological issues that can negatively affect their client rehabilitation efforts. Adequate staffing, support, and educational training may help correctional, police, peace, probation, parole, and pretrial officers therapeutically interact with those involved in the justice system. Increased client mental health-related information, education, and training may help these officers address their own as well as client-related psychologically challenging incidents, decreasing general stress and increasing therapeutic interactions for everyone involved.

Conclusion

This chapter is a detailed examination of the United States's justice system personnel, their minimum employment qualifications, and the mental health training they receive. Although many employees in the US criminal justice system possess the education and experience appropriate for their employment roles, the minimum qualifications may not in themselves be sufficient. The minimum requirements for correctional, police and court employment in the United States include being at least twenty-one years of age, being a US citizen, possessing a high school diploma or GED, having no felony convictions, being eligible to possess a firearm, being physically fit, submitting a negative drug screen, passing a background check, and possessing good interpersonal skills. Although these minimum qualifications may be enough for certain justice system positions, they may not be sufficient for higher-level interpersonal therapeutic interactions with clients.

Another current significant issue hampering the US criminal justice system is recruitment. People may not be choosing to work in the criminal justice field due to lower salaries, challenging clients, dangerous and violent employment situations, budget constraints, inadequate supervision and training, limited promotional opportunities, increased workload, mandatory overtime, and work burnout.

Although the amount of mental health education and training criminal justice system professionals actually receive may be inconsistent, it appears that increased evidence-based knowledge and instruction about how to therapeutically interact with those involved in the justice system is crucial for effective client rehabilitation. Education and training for criminal justice workers have been found to improve client rehabilitation and also correctional staff job success and satisfaction. **A growing body of research indicates that training and education are beneficial for helping justice system workers to better recognize mental health issues and support client therapeutic behavioral changes.**[44] Many of those involved in the US justice system experience challenging mental health and/or substance use disorder characteristics and might greatly benefit from correctional workers' training, knowledge, and therapeutic interactions.

National guidelines for client mental health training for criminal justice personnel have been developed by the National Commission on Correctional Health Care; however, they are voluntary and subject to federal, state, and local agency budget constraints and educational desires. It does appear from the current psychological reviews that client mental health training for correction and police officers has significantly increased over the last twenty years. At present, client mental health education frequently makes up part of the formal classroom education, academy training, Rehabilitation Methods courses, Mental Health First Aid For Public Safety classes, and Crisis Intervention Teams instruction that correctional and police officers receive. Also, "procedural justice" techniques that have been implemented by police have resulted in decreased arrests and reduced crime. It appears that future procedural justice training for police, and possibly corrections officers, has the potential to continue to yield positive results for clients. Unfortunately, without universal, national guidelines, not all criminal justice agencies are ensured to receive, at the very least, the minimum client mental health, procedural justice, or other training that may improve rehabilitation and decrease recidivism. A national mandatory implementation and accreditation of these programs by organizations like the NCCHC for justice system workers, especially for police and COs, would be expected to yield even more successful client results.

In the following chapters, suggestions will be introduced and thoroughly discussed regarding the CMC integrative approach and related therapeutic techniques. This approach may be especially beneficial to include in a course of training for justice system personnel. Evidence-based information and psychological tools for helping criminal justice staff improve their therapeutic interactions with clients will be suggested.

The evidence-based CMC integrative approach and associated psychological techniques will be discussed in detail in Chapter 6 and could become a standard for those working in the criminal justice field, especially those directly interacting with clients. More universal applications of the approach may add to recent mental health advances for those involved in the justice system. The CMC integrative approach can help justice system professionals improve their work-related success and satisfaction by enhancing client rehabilitation processes and decreasing recidivism rates.

5

Relationship-Building vs Authoritarian Personal Power Base Use

In 1959, social psychologists John R. P. French and Bertram Raven produced an influential study of power strategies, through which they developed a model categorizing five types of "power bases" associated with differing leadership styles. The framework French and Raven developed, describing ways that people can influence others, has generated extensive research in a wide range of settings. French and Raven labeled these power bases as reward, coercive, legitimate, referent, and expert. In 1965, Raven added a sixth personal base: informational power.[1] French and Raven defined power as the essential cause of receiving a desired result or compliance from another person. In 2020, Mary Kovach, PhD, produced a study titled "Leader Influence: A Research Review of French & Raven's (1959) Power Dynamics," in which she defines power as "the potential influence that one has over another person or group," and writes "generally, the one with the power has control over something the other person (or group) desires." Kovach goes on to state that a common theme in power research is that a person's behavior changes because of an influencing party.[2]

The purpose of this chapter is to examine the six personal power bases exhibited by individuals working in the US justice system, and how the use of each power base may affect clients. I will narrow these bases to focus on what I define as authoritarian vs. relationship-building personal power that individuals working in the justice system might exhibit. **The crucial importance of the "therapeutic alliance" will also be discussed in the context of a "relationship-building" style.** Based on research involving the effects of different power bases and therapy outcome literature regarding the importance of the therapeutic alliance, **I suggest that relationship-building personal power best benefits workers and clients. This would likely improve client rehabilitation and decrease recidivism while increasing employee job satisfaction.**

It is important to note that French and Raven's personal power bases appear to be unique to the individual, and it is difficult to assess if they are genetic, innate (existing from birth), and/or learned. It seems likely that some individuals are aware of their power tactics while others may not be. One of the goals of this chapter is to make criminal justice employees more aware of the individual personal power bases that they may employ. Being conscious of one's influencers allows a person to possibly choose a more therapeutic approach in a given situation.

There appears to be very limited, if any, research associated with whether French and Raven's personal power bases are genetic, innate and/or learned. As with many human psychological characteristics, it seems most likely that personal power bases may originate from genetic, innate, and environmental (learned) influences. **Leadership skills appear to be learned from experience, and thus it can be deduced that French and Raven's personal power bases can also be learned.** If that is the case, then it seems likely that people aware of their influencing ability can learn and implement a particular power base (or bases) of their choosing. Given this premise, it is my hope that justice system staff will be more aware of, and choose to implement, personal power bases that support rehabilitation.

Finally, a word about power. Power is frequently defined as the ability to do something. Oftentimes the word "power" has a negative meaning or connotation. Power can be understood as unfavorable, contrary, denying, controlling, oppressing, authoritative, corrupting, exploiting, coercing, and persuading. At other times the word "power" can have positive meanings and connotations and can be understood as inspiring, energizing, uplifting, empowering, dedicated, persisting, and/or striving. In the case of French and Raven's personal power bases, "power" can probably be best understood as a neutral concept. Several of French and Raven's personal power bases directly associated with the justice system can be characterized as more therapeutic (referent, legitimate and expert), neutral (informational), or negative (reward and coercive). For the purposes of this book, "power" itself is not meant to be defined as positive or negative, and/or healthy or unhealthy. In regard to the justice system, it is the type of personal power and how it is implemented that determines if the influencing base is therapeutic or not.

French and Raven's Six Personal Power Bases

According to researchers John French and Bertram Raven, human beings can use one or more of the six bases of personal power to influence others. These are best understood in terms of possibly genetic, innate and/or learned leadership roles. The French and Raven model lends itself well to exploring interactions that can occur in the justice system. Correctional, police, peace, parole, probation, pretrial, security, and detention officers, and line staff personnel can manifest one or more of these six bases of power while influencing the behavior of those involved in the justice system. **Thus, correctional officers (COs) aware of their personal power base options can potentially consciously exhibit one or more that may help maintain a safe institutional environment and support client rehabilitation.**

The following is a discussion of French and Raven's six personal power bases and how each one can be applied by justice system staff in performing their duties with clients.

1. **Legitimate Power**: French and Raven define "legitimate power" as a person's belief that they have the authority and right to make demands and expect others to be compliant. Legitimate power can be obtained from an employment, elected, or formal relationship position. Legitimate power influences others, for example, to follow employment rules and/or not break the law. A CO using legitimate power may believe that they are in a lawful, employment position of authority to influence clients and can expect appropriate, rule-following behavior.

   Legitimate power professionally and appropriately displayed by COs influences clients to believe that the CO is acting fairly and can justify their requests. Those involved in the justice system will respect a CO exhibiting genuine legitimate power because they believe the CO is being accountable, reasonable, honest, and trustworthy. Legitimate power can be misused and reduced if COs have unreasonable and/or unprofessional requests of clients. Additionally, those involved in the justice system may appear to be responding to a CO's legitimate power influence when, in actuality, this may not be the case. A client may decide to be compliant, not because they are responding to the CO's legitimacy, but rather due to the fear of the consequences of disobedient behavior. In that case, possible consequences would be seen as motivating behavior. Please see the discussion below on French and Raven's "coercive power base."

2. **Reward Power**: Reward power involves one person's ability to give benefits to another for compliance and/or obedience. Rewards can be personal, such as a genuine "thank you," or impersonal like a random,

abstract gift. A CO can display a reward power base when those involved in the justice system believe that if they are compliant, they will receive extra privileges. It is usually considered inappropriate for justice system staff to directly give tangible rewards to clients. COs can provide rewards including decreased chore hours, increased leisure time, and/or overlooking a rule or regulation violation.

3. **Referent Power**: French and Raven describe "referent power" as being derived from a person's perceived worthiness and attractiveness. A person's referent power comes from being respected and liked. A CO who is respected and liked by a particular person involved in the justice system may use her/his referent power to request the client be compliant. Associated with referent power, the client may be attracted to the type of person the CO is and be motivated to behave and/or think like the CO. The CO may become a role model for the client. In general, those involved in the justice system comply with a CO displaying referent power out of respect and appreciation for the CO.
4. **Expert Power**: Expert power is the influence that comes from a person's advanced competence, ability, knowledge, and/or experience about a particular subject. The person exhibiting expert power appears to be an authority on a specific subject, often making them trustworthy to others. A CO may use her/his expert power to influence a client to follow institutional rules. A person involved in the US justice system may view a CO as an expert in corrections, incarceration, the justice system, and/or problem-solving, which can include decision-making. Clients usually appreciate a genuine CO displaying expert power, value their information and/or skills, and trust the CO is trying to help them.
5. **Coercive Power**: Coercive power is a person's influence over another individual based on the belief that they can punish this person for

disorderly, noncompliant behavior. Coercion is usually considered to be forcefully influencing someone to think or behave in a certain way that they do not want to. It is forcing someone, sometimes via intimidation and/or the threat of punishment, to do something they would prefer not to do. A CO may use their coercive power, via a threat of punishment, for a client to be obedient. A CO may punish a client by decreasing their privileges, confining them to their room, and/or increasing their chore hours. Although coercion by COs may be necessary to deescalate a violent situation, it may cause clients to decrease their belief in a CO's legitimate authority power base. As stated, a legitimate personal power base originates from a justice system worker's belief that they have professional authority to make reasonable, ethical client demands. A justice system employee's coercive personal power base arises from the belief that they can forcefully influence a client to be compliant.

6. **Informational Power**: In 1965, Raven added the sixth personal power base called informational power. Informational power is described by Raven as the influence a person has based on their ability to control giving someone privileged data, facts, statistics and/or intelligence that is needed to accomplish a goal. Informational power can be acquired by an individual having the ability to obtain and give out privileged and/or confidential information. A CO may use informational power to influence a person in the justice system to be compliant. In turn, a client may be compliant in order to receive helpful privileged, goal-oriented information from a CO.[3, 4]

The US correctional system and COs have the responsibility to help rehabilitate clients. The correction system's responsibilities include implementing the criminal courts' sentencing orders, protecting the public from criminal behavior, and punishing, supervising, and providing rehabilitative treatment for clients. A CO's specific duties include enforcing rules in order to maintain a safe institutional environment, supervising, searching for contraband, resolving client and client–CO disputes, inspecting the facility, and helping to rehabilitate those involved in the justice system. The power base(s) a CO (and all other criminal justice personnel) chooses to exhibit usually has a direct effect on those involved in the justice system. Every interaction a justice system staff member has with a client has the potential to have an effect on that person. The argument can be made that the type of power base a CO displays to a client can have a negative or a therapeutic effect on that person. COs exhibiting a healthy, interpersonal power base to clients can potentially aid in their rehabilitative process.

Raven and French's power bases can be implemented when correctional, police, probation, parole, pretrial, security, and detention officers, and line staff desire to influence and manage the behavior of clients. COs put into effect the rules and regulations that are decided by their administrators. In order to maintain a safe prison, jail, halfway house, work release program, detention center, or holding facility environment, officers usually implement their power base(s) to influence those involved in the justice system to behave in a prosocial manner. French and Raven's power bases can be viewed as describing various means by which COs can help to create a safe correctional environment.

While French and Raven's concept of personal power bases appears highly relevant to exploring worker–client interactions in the justice system, actual research applying their model has been limited. In 2015, researchers Ferdik and Smith prefaced a study involving French and Raven's power base use by COs in a maximum security prison by noting, "While these power bases have been researched extensively across various academic disciplines and organizations, currently only a handful of such studies have been conducted within corrections." In Ferdik and Smith's 2015 study titled "Maximum Security Correctional Officers: An Exploratory Investigation into Their Social Bases of Power," the authors examined questionnaire data received from a

US statewide population of 559 security COs. The authors discovered that these COs rated legitimate and referent power as the most effective bases to successfully interact with those involved in the justice system. **The authors recommended that, in order to better ensure client compliance, COs can implement referent and legitimate power over other influential bases.**[5]

In 2018, a comprehensive research study was performed by Benjamin Steiner, PhD, and John Wooldredge, PhD, titled "Prison Officer Legitimacy, Their Exercise of Power, and Inmate Rule Breaking." In the authors' review of relevant research, they refer to a 1985 study done by John Hepburn, PhD, who identified that influencers employed by correction officers were consistent with the power bases that had been described by French and Raven. Steiner and Wooldredge's study goes on to acknowledge that Hepburn's research found that COs exhibit and use legitimate, referent, expert, reward, and coercive power bases to influence the behavior of those involved in the justice system. **Hepburn's research also discovered that corrections officers listed legitimate and expert power as the most influential bases resulting in clients' compliance, and reward and coercive influencers as the least important.**

Also in their 2018 research review, Steiner and Wooldredge cite other past studies indicating that when COs used legitimate, referent, and expert power, these strategies helped create an incarceration environment of mutual respect, consideration, and fairness, generally resulting in more compliant correctional facilities. COs who relied on a reward power base could promote clients' compliance only if those involved in the justice system believed they would receive some kind of benefit. **The authors also found that COs who implemented coercive power may actually encourage future client anger and disobedience.**

Steiner and Wooldredge's 2018 study, in part, also examined the general effects of CO power bases 1) as perceived by those involved in the justice system in regard to their rule breaking; and 2) on a prison's recorded

rates of client rule breaking. The study involved collecting survey data from COs and clients incarcerated for more than six months at all of Ohio's then thirty-three prisons. **The author's research found that the Ohio clients who expressed more positive opinions about the legitimacy of COs' power bases ultimately committed fewer nonviolent rule-breaking behaviors.** However, the clients' more positive opinions of the legitimacy of COs' power bases did not affect the number of violent offenses clients committed. Although it is difficult to understand how this result occurred, it is important to note that most people involved in the justice system are defined as nonviolent (See Chapter 1, "Psychological Characteristics"). **Also, Steiner and Wooldredge found that clients treated fairly and with respect during disobedient incidents ultimately had fewer subsequent nonviolent rule breakings.** The authors go on to state that this was consistent with past research findings. Interestingly, clients who were given an actual disciplinary ticket for breaking a rule committed a greater number of future nonviolent rule infractions. Perhaps those clients who received a ticket perceived this consequence as coercive and disproportionate to the situation.

Also, consistent with their review of previous research, Steiner and Wooldredge found that coercive power or force exhibited by COs was related to future disobedience and resistance from clients. The authors noted that other past research has found that when those involved in the justice system are treated with respect and fairness, less overall violence occurs in these prisons as compared to facilities implementing coercion tactics. Steiner and Wooldredge concluded that the findings of their 2018 study appeared to be consistent with past studies that found that fair and respectful treatment decreases rule-breaking behavior while coercion increases future disobedience and noncompliance.

In a 2023 study titled "Jail Officers' Adherence to Traditional Bases of Social Power: Understanding Inmate Control in a Unique Correctional Context," the authors analyzed data received from COs employed in a large urban jail.

Interestingly, the authors found that COs at this jail actually favored "coercive influence" over "referent power." Without having scientific evidence, it is difficult to understand how come this result occurred. It is important to note that this finding has generally not been reported in previous related studies.[6]

In summary, the findings from Steiner's and Wooldredge's 2018 study, and the previous research they reviewed, showed the importance of CO power base use in decreasing client rule-breaking behavior in prison. The findings strongly suggest that treating those involved in the justice system fairly and with respect may decrease future disobedient actions and increase compliant and prosocial behavior. Prisons with COs who used legitimate, referent, and expert power to influence clients had lower rule breaking behaviors than those whose COs relied on coercion. **Thus, it would be expected that when COs treat people involved in the justice system fairly, with respect, and with non-coercive power bases, they will enhance their capacity to rehabilitate clients, create safer incarceration environments, and have greater employment success and satisfaction.**[7]

French and Raven's Personal Power Bases Applied in a Psychotherapist's Practice

For those of us who work in the justice system field, French and Raven's model can provide a format for analyzing our interactions with clients. Below, I share my own experiences about how I use French and Raven's personal power bases to facilitate counseling for people involved in the justice system. I invite you, the reader, to attempt a similar process if applicable.

During my forty years of facilitating individual counseling and twenty-five years of conducting group therapy in justice system halfway houses, I have used most of French and Raven's personal power bases at one time or another. The referent power base is my most used and natural influencing style and is consistent with my personality. Referent power appears to be the closest of the bases directly associated with a psychotherapist's role in forming a "therapeutic alliance," or a professional, healthy working relationship with clients. Referent power and the therapeutic alliance strongly emphasize creating a mutually respectful psychotherapist–client relationship. Thus, many psychotherapists most likely use referent power and the therapeutic alliance in an attempt to create a healing relationship with their clients. The concept of the "therapeutic alliance" is discussed in more detail below.

Referent personal power, like all of the influencing bases, may be enhanced by a person's self-awareness. Psychotherapists and counselors are usually very interested in self-awareness and incorporate their individual personality strengths into the style of psychotherapy they practice. I am empathic by nature and the most common feedback I receive from clients is that they know that I am truly concerned about them. In general, clients have appreciated and respected me for caring. In my role as a psychotherapist, the concepts of mutual respect, appreciation, and concern seem to be the essence of a healing counselor-client therapeutic alliance.

My referent power base is usually my most therapeutic client behavior influencer and it can be accompanied by ***codependency*** *(enabling).* It is important to note that sometimes wanting to be professionally respected and seen as empathic and trustworthy by clients can cause someone relying on referent power to be unfavorably enabling. Codependency is the process of helping someone accomplish an unhealthy behavior easier than if they had attempted to do it by themselves. Accepting responsibility for a family member's, significant other's, or someone else's problematic conduct is an example of codependent behavior. A psychotherapist can potentially exhibit codependent behavior by not therapeutically confronting a client's unhealthy actions when appropriate. In general, psychotherapists who often use a personal referent power base can also benefit from being aware of the risk of exhibiting associated codependent behavior. This awareness can help psychotherapists decrease the unhealthy enabling of others. Someone who is self-aware that they are exhibiting codependent behavior can address this issue by increasing their assertiveness (see Chapter 6, "5. Assertiveness").

It is important to mention that the responsibilities of justice system psychotherapists and COs have similarities and differences. Psychotherapists facilitating counseling for those involved in the justice system usually help clients identify their psychological issues and past traumas, verbalize associated thoughts and emotions, and change problematic behaviors. Counseling can aid those involved in the justice system to recognize that they may be replicating challenging past experiences and help clients gain self-insight into their thoughts, emotions, and behaviors. Also, psychotherapists support clients in maintaining their sobriety and a prosocial lifestyle. COs can also support rehabilitation by consciously interacting with clients in a therapeutic manner. COs can intentionally attempt to create a therapeutic alliance-like relationship and make appropriate client referrals to available mental health resources. COs can offer clients support to maintain a sober, prosocial lifestyle. Both psychotherapists and COs are responsible for doing what is in the best interests of clients. COs are not responsible for the formal facilitation of counseling processes. In turn, justice system psychotherapists are not responsible for CO duties, which include enforcing rules, inspecting facilities, supervising clients, searching for contraband, and/or resolving CO–client disputes.

Additionally, I have relied on my expert personal power base when clients and justice system staff request information, knowledge, observation, research and/or therapy-related opinions from me. Often, clients place their trust in me because of my years of experience counseling those involved in the justice system. Justice system personnel have often requested my professional opinion about how to best interact with a challenging client. Justice system clients and staff have usually valued my expertise, skills, and experience.

At my discretion, I have exhibited legitimate personal power, based on my belief that as a psychotherapist I can make certain ethical and professional "requests" and expect clients to comply. I use discretion, my professional expertise to decide what will best benefit a client in a specific therapy situation when I implement legitimate or any personal power base. Being conscious of French and Raven's personal power bases allows someone to use them with discretion. Thus, I can choose to use my legitimate power when it seems to be most therapeutic. For example, I have used legitimate power to enforce group rules (e.g., being on time; one person speaks at a time; and prohibiting racial, religious, and ethnic slurs) because I believe this is in my group's best human rights interest. Group members have generally agreed that these rules were rational, fair, reasonable, and justified, and abided by them. In contrast, I employ cognitive behavioral therapy techniques (see Chapter 6, "Cognitive Behavioral Therapy Techniques") which in many psychotherapy settings usually include giving clients homework in-between individual and/or group counseling sessions. I have rarely requested that justice system clients do homework, though, because I believe that it could be counterproductive and a set-up for them not to do it. Thus, I do not use legitimate power in this homework example because I believe it would not be in my clients' best interest. I have learned this to be true by trial and error. Legitimate power, like all of the influential bases, can be used at the justice system professional's discretion.

I have occasionally used a reward personal power base with those involved in the justice system, which involves giving clients a benefit for their compliance. At my professional discretion, I have sometimes chosen not to discipline a client who broke a group rule if this person was usually compliant. I basically rewarded this client for their past compliance.

I do not use informational power, defined as being based on confidential knowledge, to influence the behavior of someone involved in the justice system. As a licensed professional counselor, I am privileged to confidential client information and bound by my professional ethics not to disclose this data unless someone is homicidal, suicidal, involved in a child or at-risk adult abuse/neglect incident, information is court ordered, or there is a threat to national security. I do give clients nonconfidential information, data, facts, and/or statistics to help them accomplish their goals.

I have very rarely used coercive power to influence someone's behavior who is involved in the justice system. Coercive power is forcing someone, sometimes via intimidation or the threat of punishment, to do something that they do not want to do. I have used coercive personal power in the very rare incidences when I have had to confront a client who has been so disruptive they interrupted the group's goal-related agenda. When this has occurred, I have requested to speak with the disruptive client individually, away from the group in order not to embarrass them. I implement the concept of praising in a group and therapeutically confronting individually and in private. I have given the disruptive client the options of either choosing to cooperatively attend group or not attend group, be reported to their case manager, and not receive group attendance credit. Even though the disruptive client would often interpret my giving them these choices as a form of punishment (coercive power), most group members supported how I handled these predicaments and understood my behavior as legitimate power.

All clients are informed in their initial individual and/or group counseling session that if they tell me they are homicidal, suicidal, or involved in a child or at-risk adult abuse/neglect incident, information is court ordered, or there is a threat to national security, I am professionally mandated to report this to the appropriate authorities, either the police or child/at-risk adult protective services. When I report these incidents and inform my clients of such, they usually interpret my reporting behavior as punishment for their being honest with me. Although informing the appropriate authorities of these issues is a mandated behavior for psychotherapists, those involved in the justice system may see being reported as a coercive measure.

The Therapeutic Alliance

The "therapeutic alliance" is defined by the American Psychological Association (APA) as "a cooperative working relationship between client [in

this case the person involved in the United States's criminal justice system] and therapist [counselor, psychotherapist, social worker, psychiatrist, psychologist, or mental health specialist] considered by many to be the essential aspect of successful therapy." The APA's definition, which was developed by psychologist Edward Bordin, PhD, (1913–92) in 1979, goes on to state that the therapeutic alliance consists of bonds, goals, and tasks. Bonds are associated with a very important aspect of psychotherapy and counseling: the client's thoughts and emotions related to the psychotherapist, and the therapist's ability to have a rapport with the person. Goals are the therapist's and client's negotiated, established, and updated as necessary, purpose(s) of psychotherapy. Tasks are the healthy behaviors implemented by the client and psychotherapist in an attempt to bring about therapeutic behavioral change.[8] Although not explicitly stated in the APA's definition, empathy, the therapist's ability to think and feel what the client is experiencing, has also been described as an essential part of this process.

The therapeutic alliance appears to be an essential element of most psychological theories, modalities, and approaches. In a 2011 study titled "Therapeutic Alliance and Outcome of Psychotherapy: Historical Excursus, Measurements, and Prospects for Research," authors R. B. Ardito and D. Rabellino explain that the concept of the "therapeutic alliance" can be understood as originating from Freud's (1913) transference theory. The authors state that the concept was later extended to other therapeutic modalities and widely used by many theorists, including Carl Rogers, who developed client-centered therapy, which will be discussed in Chapter 6. Ardito and Rabellino go on to say that Bordin's above-stated definition of the therapeutic alliance is applicable to any therapeutic approach.[9]

Psychotherapy outcome research has demonstrated the importance of the therapeutic alliance. Research has shown that the therapeutic relationship or alliance between a psychotherapist and a client is more significant in regard to a positive psychotherapy outcome than the specific

approach (e.g., psychoanalysis, client-centered, cognitive behavioral, psychodynamic, gestalt, etc.). Ardito and Rabellino go on to state that "the quality of the alliance was more predictive of positive outcome than the type of intervention."[10] A professional, ethical psychotherapist and client therapeutic alliance usually results in a positive psychotherapy outcome. Correctional psychotherapists aware of the therapeutic alliance have an opportunity to create a professional healing working relationship with those involved in the justice system.

In the 2018 book *New Frontiers in Offender Treatment: The Translation of Evidence-Based Practices to Correctional Settings, Part II*, Chapter 5, titled "The Role of the Therapeutic Alliance in Offender Therapy" (pp. 87–108), the authors B. Blasko, G. Serran, and J. Abracen address the professional working relationship between the psychotherapist and those involved in the justice system. The authors state, "In recent years, the therapeutic alliance has proven integral to treatment outcomes in offender therapy settings."[11]

Although the therapeutic alliance has been researched in regards to the relationship between mental health professionals and clients, correctional employees can also attempt to establish a healing-oriented, therapeutic alliance-like relationship with those involved in the justice system. Even though psychotherapists and other workers in the justice system operate within a context that can have unique employment challenges, all correctional employees can play an important role in the delivery of mental health-related services to those involved in the justice system. Justice system personnel aware of the evidence-based healing, therapeutic alliance-like relationship can implement such with willing clients.

I am suggesting that correctional, police, peace, probation, parole, pretrial, security, and detention officers, and anyone else working in the justice system, can create a therapeutic alliance-like relationship with

those involved in the justice system. Officers can focus on correctional environmental safety, and other employees can pay attention to their specific work responsibilities, while they all simultaneously attend to the rehabilitation of clients by offering information, support, and motivation. Every interaction with a client can have a therapeutic effect.

Integrating French and Raven's Personal Power Bases and the Therapeutic Alliance

The research on personal power bases and literature confirming the importance of a therapeutic alliance support the use of healing interpersonal approaches for criminal justice system workers. Research associated with French and Raven's model suggests that referent, legitimate and expert personal power bases promote a greater sense of mutual respect, while coercive and reward influencers tend to be significantly less successful. Also, a therapeutic alliance-like relationship can be highly effective in encouraging those involved in the justice system to establish, and ultimately maintain, a prosocial lifestyle. Taken together, research on personal power bases and the therapeutic alliance can be viewed as supporting the implementation of this combination of powerful rehabilitative treatment approaches.

Justice system personnel attempting to create an empathic therapeutic alliance-like relationship and combining it with an effective power base can actively aid in a client's rehabilitation. The therapeutic alliance supports, motivates, informs, educates, and helps build trust. A therapeutic power base can help clients think and feel that they are being treated fairly, justly, and respectfully. Justice system personnel implementing an effective personal power base and alliance can decrease recidivism and increase employment success and satisfaction.

Conclusion

French and Raven's personal power base model has been supported by the associated research that followed their work as noted in this chapter. Combining French and Raven's personal power base findings with the information supporting the therapeutic alliance encourages the use of healthy "relationship-building" techniques when interacting with those involved in the justice system. French and Raven's legitimate, referent, and expert personal power bases in combination with the therapeutic alliance (relationship-building personal power) would be expected to influence clients to believe that the CO is acting empathically, fairly, honestly, reasonably, rationally, and respectfully. Research noted in this chapter also provides confirmation that what I am now labeling as **"relationship-building personal power"** may create more client-compliant and effective correctional facilities.

French and Raven's coercive personal power base seems consistent with an approach that an authoritarian and/or militaristic type of CO, or system, might employ with eventual negative results. Coercion usually refers to forcing those involved in the justice system to do something they do not want to do. The authoritarian CO would be inclined to believe that the threat of punishing clients for disorderly behavior influences them to be compliant. While coercion may be necessary to deescalate a violent incident, authoritarian COs may often lose their legitimacy with those involved in the justice system as a consequence of their discretionary use of punishment. Authoritarian COs who coerce clients can encourage future noncompliance, anger, and disobedience.

COs, and anyone working in the criminal justice field, can attempt to create a therapeutic alliance-like professional relationship with those involved in the justice system. All justice system workers can play an essential role in the delivery of mental health type services to clients. By creating a therapeutic alliance-like relationship, the entire justice system workforce can help support, encourage, and motivate those involved in the justice system to adhere to correctional facility rules and ultimately establish a prosocial lifestyle.

Combining French and Raven's legitimate, referent, and/or expert personal power base(s) with a therapeutic alliance-like relationship has the capability to encourage significant client change and improved rehabilitation. This relationship-building approach has the potential to increase client-compliant behavior, produce more secure correctional environments, improve rehabilitation efforts, and decrease recidivism.

6

An Integrative Approach

Creating a Therapeutic Alliance Between Criminal Justice Workers and People Involved in the Justice System

The CMC Integrative Approach

It is my belief that if criminal justice workers can use this book to learn about and implement a combination of established evidence-based therapies, they can provide the rehabilitative alliance (relationship) necessary to support people in the justice system. The term therapeutic alliance is most commonly used to describe the working relationship created between a psychotherapist and a client. Studies have shown that a successful client-therapist relationship results in a positive, healing outcome. It appears that a therapeutic relationship between criminal justice workers and those involved in the justice system supports the latter in establishing a prosocial lifestyle. Client-centered therapy (CCT) proposes that a therapeutic relationship can lead to client insight and change. Motivational interviewing (MI) strongly supports counselors establishing a therapeutic alliance with clients and is an approach that helps people process their ambivalence and promotes prosocial behavior change. Cognitive behavioral therapy (CBT) supports therapists and clients in creating a strong working relationship in order to help the latter change irrational thoughts and behaviors to rational beliefs and actions, while promoting success-oriented problem-solving skills. **Combined, these therapeutic relationship-oriented approaches have the potential to expedite and increase client rehabilitation.**

I have named this concept the **CMC integrative approach**. This name is derived from the first letter of CCT (C), MI (M), and CBT (C). Integrative in this case means combined. Approach is defined as a method intended to problem-solve an issue. The CMC integrative approach combines three evidence-based therapies.

The CMC integrative approach is a new method in that it combines evidence-based CCT, MI and CBT processes and therapeutic interventions. The CMC method in itself is not a new psychological theory and/or intervention.

The CMC integrative approach can aid clients in establishing successful, prosocial lifestyles. If criminal justice workers can learn and implement the basics of the approach, it is my belief that they can help give willing clients the respect, dignity, support, psychological foundation, and skills necessary to improve rehabilitation. It is important to note that I am not suggesting that everyone employed in criminal justice-related work become experts in CCT, MI, and CBT. Each of these therapies takes years to learn and put into practice. Nor am I proposing that this book is a thorough examination of these therapies, as each discipline is the subject of many books. An extensive review of these therapies is not within the scope or goal of this book. What I will attempt to do is give you, the reader, a simplified overview of how to learn about, combine, and implement these therapies and techniques to create a healing alliance with those involved in the justice system. Previous chapters of this book have established that a relationship-building criminal justice worker–client alliance can promote successful outcomes.

Client-Centered Therapy (CCT)

Carl Rogers developed CCT, also known as Rogerian and person-centered therapy, in the 1940s and 1950s. It is a form of talk therapy in which the client and therapist are considered equals. The therapist utilizes empathy: the ability of one person to try to feel what another person is emotionally experiencing. Clients are believed to be experts about their own lives and control the focus and pace of their therapy sessions. Rogers believed that clients attempt to "self-actualize" to try to achieve their goal of being the best version of themselves. *Often, in their initial individual counseling session with me, clients have verbalized that their goal is "to be the best person" they can be.* Even though Rogers wanted CCT to be non-directive, he also believed that therapists guide clients, and that clients expect such. The philosophy of CCT supports the idea that individuals have the potential to gain self-insight, improve their self-concept, and change behaviors therapeutically by establishing a healthy relationship with their therapist.[1]

If criminal justice workers can establish healthy relationships and implement CCT techniques with people involved in the justice system, rehabilitation efforts may be significantly improved. Rogers believed that therapists need to exhibit unconditional positive regard, empathic understanding, and genuineness (also called congruence) in their relationships with clients to help them be more self-aware and make behavioral changes. He proposed that therapists needed to help clients focus on their conscious thoughts, feelings, and behaviors. Unconditional positive regard is acceptance of who the client is and supporting them when professionally appropriate. Empathic understanding is the ability to experience the thoughts and feelings of clients to help them better understand themselves. It is also important for client-centered advocates to listen to and accept challenging emotions exhibited by clients. People involved in the justice system often express anger toward criminal justice workers in unhealthy ways. Although very challenging, it is important for criminal justice workers to attempt not to personalize a client's anger. Oftentimes, clients project (place) their general anger at the criminal justice system and themselves onto justice workers. Genuineness is the technique in which the criminal justice professional authentically shares with the client, exhibiting that all people experience similar human states, emotions, thoughts, and behaviors. This technique helps clients recognize that we are all part of humanity and find a realistic balance between who they actually are (real self) and how they can strive to become the best version of themselves (ideal self).[2]

I received my Master of Arts Degree in Counseling Psychology at the University of Northern Colorado in 1985. The focus of my master's degree was Rogerian and Carkhuffian in nature. Robert R. Carkhuff is a psychologist who was a student of Carl Rogers and strongly supports the psychological idea that human growth and development is all about relating interpersonally (between people).[3] Carkhuff expanded on Roger's work to emphasize how essential interpersonal relationships are in healing people. Many experts in the psychological community believe that the therapeutic relationship between the client and therapist is a significant healing factor. *In my current individual counseling sessions, as well as twenty-five years of facilitating alcohol/drug relapse prevention and life skills/transition groups in justice system halfway houses, I found that the most important skills I utilize are empathy, caring, and genuine concern for my clients. Treating clients with dignity and respect, and in the way I want to be treated, usually helps us build a trusting and healing relationship. I also know this from feedback received from individuals upon successful graduation from group. Often, a client graduating from group has said, "I know you care, Howie." This reinforces for me Roger's and Carkhuff's belief that genuine interpersonal relationships help people heal. Teaching clients relapse prevention, life skills, anger management, parenting, assertiveness, problem-solving, decision-making, victim impact and mindfulness is easier once the client knows that you genuinely care.*

Person-centered therapy is an evidence-based practice, which means that it is supported by scientific research. In 2008, Isabel Gibbard and Terry Hanley, PhD, published their study titled "A Five Year Evaluation of the Effectiveness of Person-centered Counselling in Routine Clinical Practice in Primary Care." This study involved 1,079 subjects. The authors found that person-centered therapy is effective for clients with common mental health issues, including anxiety and depression. The study also discovered that person-centered therapy's effectiveness extended to people who had moderate to severe psychological symptoms.[4]

In 2019, Mick Cooper, psychologist and Director of the Centre for Social and Psychological Transformation at the University of Roehampton, London[5] wrote an article titled "Is Person-Centered Therapy Effective? The Facts" supporting CCT. In this article, Cooper outlined ten facts supporting the therapeutic effectiveness of person-centered therapy. Cooper's article also stated that person-centered therapy treatment success is similar to the positive results of CBT.[6]

Motivational Interviewing (MI)

According to Jill Stinson, PhD, and Michael Clark, MSW, authors of the book *Motivational Interviewing with Offenders*, "MI is, first and foremost, a way of being with people." The authors go on to say that MI promotes criminal justice workers to be themselves and build a professional, ethical relationship (therapeutic alliance) with clients based on "motivation, respect and meaningful change."[7] MI is a method for criminal justice workers to interact with people in the justice system in a way in which clients can evaluate their past antisocial behavior and associated consequences using rational thinking. A criminal justice worker using MI might sincerely ask a client "How did that behavior work for you?" If the answer is negative, a willing client can then be gently guided to attempt to identify other alternatives to the problematic behavior and decide for themselves if a prosocial option will work better in the future.

This is not meant to be a comprehensive, in-depth description of MI. MI is a detailed, therapeutic approach whose facilitators receive thorough training in helping ambivalent clients make therapeutic behavioral changes. I am advocating that if criminal justice workers can implement the described basic MI techniques, they will be increasing therapeutic interactions with those under correctional supervision.

MI was developed by psychologists William Miller and Stephen Rollnick in 1983. Miller and Rollnick wrote in 2013 that "MI is a collaborative, goal-oriented style of communication with particular attention to the language of change. It is designed to strengthen personal motivation for and commitment to a specific goal by eliciting and exploring the person's own reasons for change within an atmosphere of acceptance and compassion."[8] MI is an empathic, somewhat directive, person-centered process which helps people in the justice system resolve ambivalence and consider prosocial behavior alternatives. MI practitioners interact with clients as equals and do not warn, direct, instruct, confront, or give unwanted advice.[9] Instead, criminal justice workers implementing MI can use open-ended questions, affirmations, reflections, summaries, and prosocial change talk to help clients consider making therapeutic advances. Open-ended questions do not elicit yes or no answers and help clients discuss the positives and negatives of change. "How?" and "How come?" are effective ways to ask open-ended questions. Giving affirmations, encouragement, and making positive statements is a way to support a client's prosocial behavior consideration. Reflecting back, rephrasing, and/or repeating what a client says is a way of showing one is listening and attempting to be empathic. When a listener summarizes what a person says, they exhibit understanding and highlight the important points that were made. Finally, supporting, encouraging, and contributing to prosocial change talk exhibited by the person involved in the justice system can help them seriously consider choosing future healthy behaviors.[10]

MI is a respectful discussion between at least two people, which encourages one person's desire to change. The criminal justice professional implementing MI techniques needs to be able to express empathy as previously stated, promote client self-efficacy, accept verbal confrontation, and help people explore their thought and behavior inconsistencies. Empathy involves the criminal justice professional's ability to appreciate the client's thoughts, feelings, and experiences. Self-efficacy is defined by psychologist Albert Bandura, PhD, as an individual's belief about their ability to implement behaviors necessary to attain their goals[11]. A criminal justice professional can help people involved in the justice system by supporting their belief that they can achieve their prosocial goals. MI supports criminal justice professionals not confronting a client's resistance and instead communicating in a manner to avoid negative interactions. This MI technique is called "rolling with it." "Rolling with it" is used to avoid the negative consequences of power struggles resulting in a win–lose outcome. No one likes to lose. Loss is usually associated with grief and can trigger challenging emotions, including anger, sadness, depression, and anxiety. MI also promotes a person defining and problem-solving issues, with the criminal justice professional suggesting that the client consider new, prosocial points of view and behaviors. Motivation for prosocial change occurs when a person becomes aware of the inconsistencies between their real (who they currently are) and ideal (who they ultimately want to be) selves, a la Carl Rogers. MI also incorporates the use of the Transtheoretical Model of behavioral change (TTM), also called The Stages of Change (please refer to Chapter 3). MI encourages the criminal justice worker to attempt to identify the stage of change a client is in and then utilize the most effective strategies (see below). A criminal justice professional implementing MI helps clients recognize the inconsistencies of their past antisocial activities (leading to negative consequences) and their desire to pursue positive outcome prosocial behaviors.[12]

Research indicates that MI is a very successful, evidence-based counseling approach.[13] If criminal justice workers interacting with clients can implement these basic MI concepts and skills, they can help them confront their ambivalence and consider prosocial lifestyle choices.

Cognitive Behavioral Therapy (CBT)

According to the American Psychological Association, CBT is a form of psychological counseling that is effective in treating anxiety, depression, substance use disorder, and a wide variety of mental health issues. Evidence-based treatment studies strongly suggest that CBT significantly improves a person's quality of life and is as (or more) effective than other forms of psychological treatment.[14]

Aaron Beck, MD, is usually considered to be the father of CBT. Beck was a psychoanalyst and prolific researcher who sought evidence-based psychological techniques to help his depressed and anxious clients. Beck's research led him to develop CBT in the 1960s. The basic premise of CBT is that challenging emotions may be the result of irrational thoughts. Changing irrational ideas to rational thoughts and behaviors decreases the intensity of challenging emotions.

CBT supports the belief that psychological issues are caused by irrational thinking and learned associated inadequate behaviors. CBT suggests that dysfunctional thoughts, beliefs, and attitudes can lead to inappropriate, inadequate, and/or destructive behavior. People involved in the justice system often use irrational thinking to explain their antisocial actions, which can help maintain such behavior. Changing these cognitive distortions can lead to constructive, prosocial behavior. CBT advocates that people with psychological issues can learn skills to manage their thinking errors and problematic behaviors and may decrease their associated challenging emotions. CBT rational thinking techniques help people learn to identify their cognitive distortions and associated challenging emotions, reevaluate them, and replace them with rational thoughts, often decreasing anxiety and depression. CBT helps people therapeutically confront issues, practice mindfulness (awareness), and use problem-solving skills, like assertiveness, to change problematic behaviors. In CBT, the client and therapist work together to assess the client's issues and create a problem-solving treatment plan.[15]

A 2007 systematic review by Mark Lipsey, PhD, Nana Landenberger, and Sandra Wilson titled "The Effects of Cognitive-Behavioral Programs for Criminal Offenders" concluded that CBT can prevent clients from engaging in future crimes. This review of CBT studies showed that the specific CBT treatment needed to be precisely implemented by a thoroughly trained facilitator. In other words, CBT taught by trained people can help clients involved in the justice system decrease their possible future criminal behaviors.[16]

Again, I am not suggesting people employed in a criminal justice-related profession interacting with clients be experts in CBT. *In my forty years of counseling, I continue to learn about new CBT concepts and techniques to help clients be more successful.* I am suggesting that if criminal justice workers can successfully learn and implement the very basic techniques of CBT, they can help those who are incarcerated, on probation or parole lead more prosocial lifestyles.

Before examining CBT skills, techniques, and interventions, it is essential to discuss the need for precise client evaluation. Accurately assessing those involved in the justice system can improve rehabilitation efforts and decrease recidivism.

Client Assessment

The Risk-Need-Responsivity (RNR) Model of client assessment is an evidence-based set of principles widely used in the US criminal justice

system to evaluate a client's risk to reoffend and treatment needs. The RNR Model provides a structured approach that can improve client rehabilitation through individualized intervention suggestions and decrease recidivism. Client information for the RNR model can be gathered through a presentence investigation, evidence-based assessments, monitoring, interviews, and communication.

The RNR "risk" principle addresses the client's likelihood of reoffending. The risk principle supports the concept that a client's risk of committing a future crime determines their level of treatment. Higher risk clients receive more intensive levels of treatment than lower risk individuals.

The "need" concept addresses the client's specific treatment needs (e.g., anger management, substance use disorder counseling). Adequately addressing a client's treatment needs can decrease their likelihood of reoffending.

The "responsivity" idea focuses on how to effectively administer a client's treatment by taking into account their motivation and capabilities. This requires adjusting client interventions to their abilities.

The Level of Service Inventory-Revised (LSI-R) is an evidence-based risk assessment instrument widely used in conjunction with the RNR. The LSI-R is a tool that evaluates a client's risk to reoffend and identifies their treatment needs. The LSI-R gives clients a risk of recidivism score and identifies treatment interventions that the client can best benefit from. Like the RNR, the LSI-R takes into account a client's risk, need, and responsivity.

The RNR and the LSI-R are often used together with the goals of reducing recidivism and improving client rehabilitation. While the RNR is a set of principles and concepts, the LSI-R is a specific assessment tool used in the RNR framework. The LSI-R is an instrument that implements the RNR Model. Together the RNR and LSI-R can produce an evidence-based assessment of clients.[17]

Cognitive Behavioral Therapy Techniques

CBT-oriented techniques include, and are not limited to, psychological suggestion, rational thinking, decision-making, problem-solving, assertiveness, alcohol/drug relapse (recurrence) prevention, anger management, victim impact, mindfulness, meditation, positive thinking, practicing gratitude, and parenting. It is also important for criminal justice professionals to recognize that they can choose to be therapeutic role models for people involved in the justice system. Awareness of the transition process and The Stages of Change (see Chapter 3, "The Transtheoretical Model [TTM]—The Stages of Change") can support clients who are pursuing successful sentence completion and prosocial lifestyles. Finally, criminal justice workers can best learn and implement these techniques by generating discussion, asking questions, and sharing information in a collaborative manner and not telling clients what to do.

The foundation of the CMC integrative approach can be established after assessing a client and starting to implement CCT, MI, and CBT methods and associated suggested interventions. Implementing the CMC integrative approach, which includes the CBT interventions described below, may significantly improve client rehabilitation.

1. Psychological Suggestion

The American Psychological Association's Dictionary of Psychology defines suggestion as "an idea or potential course of action presented to another for consideration."[18] In a research paper titled "Suggestion, Cognition, and Behavior," 2012, Robert B. Michael, Maryanne Garry, and Irving Kirsch reviewed research that claims deliberate and nondeliberate suggestions can influence a person's thoughts and behaviors. The authors cite evidence-based research that concludes suggestions can be helpful or harmful, as they tend to bring about the implied expectation. A person's suggestions can create a client's response expectancies, which is what people anticipate their replies are going to be in a specific situation. A person's response expectancy includes the outcome a client anticipates if they reply in a certain way. When we expect a particular result, we activate thoughts and behaviors to produce that result. Basically, when we anticipate an outcome, our thoughts and behaviors attempt to bring it about. If we choose to take a supplement we are told can strengthen our knees, we will likely report our joints feel better. This is also known as the placebo effect.

The American Psychological Association's APA Dictionary of Psychology defines the placebo effect as

> **a clinically significant response to a therapeutically inert substance or nonspecific treatment (placebo), deriving from the recipient's expectations or beliefs regarding the intervention. It is now recognized that placebo effects accompany the administration of any drug (active or inert) and contribute to the therapeutic effectiveness of a specific treatment. For example, patients given a placebo to relieve headaches may report statistically significant reductions in headaches in studies that compare them with patients who receive no treatment at all. This term is also used more generally in nonclinical studies to indicate any effect arising from a participant's expectations regarding the study.**[19]

Thus, if it is suggested to us that a particular behavior will bring about a desired result, that outcome is likely to occur. Studies have shown that if a person is informed that sniffing a scented cotton ball will bring about faster or slower results, it does. If a client receives a trusted correctional officer's suggestion that compliant actions will help them complete their sentence more efficiently, the individual will activate thoughts and behaviors to be prosocial in an attempt to achieve the desired result. What we expect to occur makes us think and behave in a way to bring about our expectations, usually the desired result. The immediately above-stated authors conclude, "If we can harness the power of suggestion, we can improve people's lives."[20]

So, how do we harness the power of suggestion? According to the above-stated research, suggestions influence how people respond. Some of the newly emphasized variety of CBT-related practices, which include positive thinking, mindfulness (presence without judgment), gratitude, and meditation are relatively easy, little or no financial cost skills for someone to acquire and implement. Correctional officers can therapeutically suggest that clients use positive thinking, mindfulness, gratitude, and meditation to help them decrease anxiety and/or depression.

I define positive suggestion as someone giving another person an idea or example of a behavior that focuses on a good, or the best possible outcome of a situation. I would go as far as to say that positive suggestion includes rationally understanding a defeat by focusing on what good results from the outcome. We see this often in sporting competitions in which the coach helps her/his team learn from mistakes that resulted in their defeat.

Consciously using positive suggestions with clients appears to be a technique that can be easily learned by justice system professionals and may have a significant impact on a client's success. A justice system professional giving a positive suggestion to a client appears to be a conscious, simple, therapeutic technique that will most likely help with the client's success and rehabilitation.

How willing are people under correctional supervision to listen to and accept therapeutic psychological suggestions? I have not been able to locate research addressing the concept of making therapeutic suggestions to those involved in the justice system. *My personal observations are that clients are often quite willing to accept positive suggestions. I have observed that clients can usually recognize the consequences of their antisocial behavior. Offering prosocial suggestions after a client recognizes their consequences may motivate rational thinking and help an individual decide to change antisocial actions to prosocial behaviors.*

When we take into account the information that was discussed in Chapter 1 in the section "Psychological Characteristics" of those involved in the justice system, as well as in Chapter 3 in the section "Psychological Reactance," it leads us to believe that those involved in the justice system may not be very amenable to psychological suggestion. As previously stated, those involved in the justice system usually have ASPD characteristics that may include irresponsibility, manipulation, dishonesty, irrational thinking, charm, narcissism, impulsivity, being unremorseful, having a lack of empathy, and blaming. Combined with psychological reactance, which can make a client strongly respond to a threat of losing a freedom in a noncompliant manner, it seems logical to believe those under correctional supervision are not the best candidates to accept therapeutic psychological suggestions. Those under correctional supervision, like most people, do not like being told what to do unless they are soliciting advice. Also, it is important to note that sometimes correctional officers don't accept the responsibility of rehabilitating clients.

This information might make criminal justice professionals ask themselves and their colleagues, "Is it worth making the effort to give positive, therapeutic psychological suggestions to clients?" The answer is absolutely yes. The positive psychology movement, led by psychologist Martin Seligman, has produced a wide variety of evidence-based studies indicating that optimism, positive thinking, and helping others benefit the giver and the receiver. Simply stated, it is a win-win situation for justice system workers and those under correctional supervision. In a 2022 research study titled "Positive Psychological Suggestions Improve the Self-Efficacy, Social Functioning and Mood of Patients Undergoing Replantation," the authors studied people who received reinsertion of bodily parts (limbs, teeth). The authors discovered that positive psychological suggestions improved patients' self-efficacy (a person's belief in their ability to engage in behaviors needed to achieve their goals), social functioning, and mood.[21] In a 2020 meta-analysis (a statistical review combining the results of many significant studies), the authors discovered that there is a moderate association between prosocial behavior and well-being.[22] A prosocial behavior can include making positive psychological suggestions to another person. This could involve justice system professionals and staff being taught to make conscious positive psychological suggestions to those involved in the justice system. The win-win that exists here is that criminal justice professionals making positive psychological suggestions to clients can improve their own general good health by helping others, while those involved in the justice system receiving these ideas can enhance their self-efficacy, social functioning, and emotional state.

It appears that the US justice system has a good chance of successfully improving rehabilitation efforts if correctional professionals and clients can benefit from the implementation of general positive therapeutic techniques. Positive psychological suggestions improve a client's ability to believe that they can achieve their prosocial goals. Justice system workers making positive psychological suggestions can improve their general well-being and success rates by doing so.

2. Rational Thinking

According to CBT, irrational thinking can be generally defined as illogical, inadequate, distorted, impulsive, and non-thorough reasoning. Irrational thinking can often originate in childhood from beliefs arising from a person's family of origin, and/or from past trauma, and then be triggered by a current situation. *For example, during childhood, my father would compare my grades to those of my best friend who was a straight A student, causing me to believe I was inadequate when I didn't receive excellent marks. "Why didn't you do as well in school as your best friend?" my father would ask. This inquiry caused me to believe I was not very smart, and I would feel sad, anxious, guilty, and angry. In my early adulthood, an experience that seemed to me to be a failure would trigger an inadequate belief and associated emotions. This would be exacerbated by my childhood experience of believing I was inadequate and trigger excess feelings of sadness, depression, guilt and anger. When I received a C in a very competitive college freshman biology introduction course, I was devastated and thought I truly was inadequate. I had overwhelming feelings of sadness, depression, guilt, and anger. No doubt my being overwhelmed emotionally and thoughts of insufficiency were a culmination of my grade, the message I received from my father in childhood that I was inadequate, and my internalized belief that I was. Understanding this allowed me to begin the process of challenging irrational thoughts with rational thinking by focusing on facts and my successes, decreasing difficult emotions.*

Irrational thinking can also occur when a person has low self-esteem, experiences trauma, or fails at an endeavor. Emotional consequences may include excessive anger, sadness, depression, guilt, grief, and/or anxiety. Anticipation, or contemplating beforehand how a prospective situation might have negative consequences without having to actually experience it, is a form of rational thinking that can help a client navigate possible future challenging circumstances. Rational, positive, factual, anticipatory thinking helps people decrease emotional consequences by directly confronting irrational thoughts.[23]

Criminal justice workers who witness a client exhibiting irrational thinking can help a willing listener by suggesting such reasoning may be faulty and harmful and result in negative consequences. Suggesting that a client take a deep breath, slow down their thinking process, and replace negative, irrational thoughts with positive, factual, rational thinking can help someone decrease challenging emotions.

3. Decision-Making

Decision-making is another cognitive skill associated with rational and critical thinking that a criminal justice worker can help teach. Critical thinking has several definitions. Critical thinking for CBT purposes can be defined as logical, evidence-based, rational thinking. A halfway house line staff member could suggest that a client, struggling to make a choice between available options, create a running list of the positive and negative results of making a particular decision. Then the staff member can suggest that the client assign a weight score of one to ten to all listed items, based on how important each result is to the client. The more important the item, the higher the weight score. A line staff member could also suggest to a client that they share their decision-making process and their positive and negative lists with a trusted person in order to receive feedback and possibly discover any missed results. Adding up the positive and negative assigned points, the side with the highest score helps indicate a better decision. This decision-making technique can help clients make the most rational, thought-out decision.

4. Problem-Solving

Criminal justice workers can assist clients with problem-solving by helping them recognize their possible situational options and using the above combination of rational thinking and decision-making skills to choose their best solution. Rational thinking combined with decision-making involves helping a client slow down their thoughts and choose the most logical option, possibly causing a lesser degree of consequences and challenging emotions (anger, sadness, depression, disappointment, guilt, and/or grief). It is not the criminal justice worker's responsibility to problem-solve, think rationally, or make decisions for the client. Justice system workers can potentially help a willing client accept and respect their emotions and be more aware of their prosocial rational thoughts, options, behaviors, and solutions.

5. Assertiveness

Assertiveness is one of the most important and beneficial skills I have taught people involved in the justice system. Using assertiveness skills, clients can pursue their reasonable needs and wants in a prosocial manner. Assertiveness is the skill of asking for what one wants and/or needs, while taking into consideration the thoughts, feelings, and desires of the person(s) they are interacting with. Assertiveness often involves compromising to establish a mutual agreement between the parties involved. Assertiveness is limit and boundary setting, and/or saying no when a person cannot do what is requested. Assertiveness also entails the use of therapeutic confrontation (direct communication), conflict resolution, and implementing the statement "I feel (insert emotion) because (insert reason) and I would like (insert solution)" when a person is experiencing a controversy with someone else. Assertiveness involves thinking about oneself positively, stating disagreements as calmly as possible, seeking fair treatment, using "I" messages, listening, and accepting that all human beings make mistakes. Assertiveness is not being passive, allowing other people to decide for you without your input. Assertiveness is not being aggressive, pursuing what you want without taking other people's thoughts, feelings, or wants into consideration. Assertiveness is not exhibiting passive-aggressive behavior, which is an indirect expression of anger (e.g., the silent treatment, procrastination, and/or sarcasm). If criminal justice workers can help willing clients learn to be more assertive by discussing the above guidelines, they can support them in developing an essential prosocial life-skill.[24]

6. Alcohol/Drug Relapse (Recurrence) Prevention

Relapse prevention, also known as recurrence prevention, is a CBT skill that can help clients establish and maintain alcohol/drug sobriety at least while involved in the criminal justice system and possibly for the rest of their lives. It is important to emphasize that along with antisocial personality disorder characteristics, approximately 85 percent of the United States' prison population may also have alcohol/drug-related issues. **The majority of those who are incarcerated, on parole, or probation have substance use issues** (see Chapter 1, "Psychological Characteristics").

Relapse can be defined as making a commitment to change a behavior and breaking that commitment. *Most people I have counseled who are under correctional supervision have expressed a desire to be alcohol/drug sober at least while they are in the system. Many clients I have encountered have a strong desire to comply and complete their justice system sentence as quickly as possible.* A criminal justice worker's basic knowledge of alcohol/drug triggers, high-risk relapse situations, how to not use substances in challenging predicaments, and how to establish and preserve a sober lifestyle can be constructively shared with willing clients who are attempting to maintain sobriety. Alcohol/drug relapse prevention information is straightforward and manageable for justice system staff to learn and dispense to clients.

An alcohol/drug trigger is anything that increases a person's risk to use substances.[25] Facilitating substance use and relapse prevention groups at justice system halfway houses, I observed most clients' triggers included, yet were not limited to, people, places, and things associated with alcohol/drugs, cravings, a desire to alter one's state of consciousness, lifestyle changes (e.g., moving, loss of employment, death of an important person, etc.), a desire to "have fun," general stress from a variety of sources, boredom, irrational thinking, and challenging emotions (e.g., sadness, depression, grief, anxiety, guilt, and anger).

High-risk alcohol/drug relapse situations are triggers and usually places that increase a person's risk of using substances. High-risk relapse situations include, yet are not limited to, bars, clubs, liquor stores, marijuana dispensaries, family gatherings, concerts, public parks, parties, and any place where drugs and alcohol are being used or sold. It is best for clients to avoid high-risk alcohol/drug relapse situations, if possible, to reduce their risk of recurrence.

When people involved in the justice system find themselves in a high-risk alcohol/drug relapse situation, usually their best response is to immediately leave in order to remain sober. If they choose to stay in that situation for whatever reason, clients can say no to alcohol/drugs and/or use rational thinking (asking themselves "What will my consequences be if I use drugs/alcohol?") and/or prayer, if they are spiritual, to remain sober. The longer one remains in a high-risk relapse situation, the more likely their urges will increase and/or keep returning, and the greater the possibility for a relapse to occur. If a client leaves a high-risk relapse situation and experiences alcohol/drug cravings, they can contact someone in their support system (e.g., family, friend, clergy, sponsor, or therapist) to talk with until their alcohol/drug urges pass.

Clients have reported to me that most alcohol/drug urges will subside in five to ten minutes, although they may return quickly thereafter. I often suggest that clients experiencing an alcohol/drug craving attempt to close their eyes and visualize themselves standing on a surfboard atop a wave (symbolic of an urge) and riding the crest to the shoreline (representative of a decreasing craving). This visualization technique is called "surfing the urge." Remembering alcohol/drug use consequences can help someone say no to alcohol/drugs and/or leave a high-risk relapse situation. If clients can use the rational thinking skill of anticipating the possible negative consequences of a high-risk relapse situation, they may choose to avoid it altogether. Justice system workers knowledgeable of this information can inform clients about how to maintain their sobriety while they are in the system. Ordering and/or telling clients what to do often doesn't work. Medical doctors have all told cigarette smokers to stop smoking, yet many continue this behavior. As mentioned in Chapter 3, psychological reactance may cause this response. Generating a discussion, asking a client how a behavior is working for them (MI), and sharing information in a respectful manner encourages people to therapeutically contemplate their actions and possible prosocial solutions.

Most of my clients who have succeeded in maintaining alcohol/drug sobriety do so by establishing a prosocial lifestyle. I define prosocial as being a moral, active, positive, employed (if able and not retired), contributing member of society who is not engaging in criminal behavior. I define lifestyle as a manner of living that incorporates meeting a person's occupational, social, physical, psychological, financial, spiritual, intellectual, environmental, and emotional needs. This idea is based on Dr. Bill Hettler's Wellness Wheel, which suggests that a healthy lifestyle can be attained by attempting to balance many of these concepts.[26] Lifestyle balance can be difficult to attain due to ever-changing individual life events and societal demands.

The establishment of sobriety and a prosocial lifestyle seems to go hand in hand and therapeutically feed off each other. A sobriety plan, incorporating what has already been discussed with the addition of answering the question "How will I stay sober on a daily basis?" seems essential. The ingredients of a sobriety plan may include, yet are not limited to, employment, exercise, Alcoholics/Narcotics/Cocaine Anonymous, spirituality, a sense of purpose, reading, journaling, gratitude, socializing, individual/group counseling, playing sports, medication, music engagement, meditation, adequate sleep, healthy diet, mindfulness, and prosocial family/friend interaction. This idea is very similar to what Bill Hettler believed was a wellness-oriented lifestyle. These sobriety plan "ingredients" also seem to lend themselves to decreasing the general human stress reaction, also known as the fight-or-flight response. When a person recognizes a significant threat, the fight-or-flight physiological automatic response occurs, possibly increasing heart rate, breathing speed, blood pressure, adrenaline, cortisol, and sweating, as well as other physical symptoms. This allows people to either directly confront or escape a threatening situation. The stressful nature of many people's lives seems to trigger the emergency fight-or-flight response even when the situation may not warrant it. Over an extended period of time, an overreactive tension response may cause toxic stress, which can have negative physical and psychological effects on the human body (see Chapter 1, "Adverse Childhood Experiences [ACEs]").[27] If a person can consistently engage in some of the above-stated self-care activities, they may improve their chances of avoiding an unnecessary fight-or-flight response and ultimately maintain a sober, prosocial, and healthier lifestyle. If criminal justice workers can support willing clients in managing their sobriety plan, they may help them establish successful lives.

7. Anger Management

Men may express anger when they actually want to communicate other emotions that can make them appear vulnerable, because it is more socially acceptable. *In the late 1980s, I facilitated an anger management and substance use group for men convicted of domestic violence. During this time, I learned that for many men, anger is an umbrella emotion, the first line of defense for them to express a socially acceptable feeling. Even though sadness, depression, guilt, and anxiety might lie under one's anger, these emotions were difficult for men to label and usually not expressed to others for fear of appearing vulnerable.* Many male children receive society's message that they need to be strong physically, mentally, and emotionally. Some parents encourage male children to be strong, tough, and resilient and not to cry, be sad, or depressed. *Being a child of the 1960s, I experienced the then progressive male movement as informing boys that it was okay to be sad, depressed, and anxious, and to express these emotions through talking.* Then, it appeared as if this new male socialization movement of the 1960s and early 1970s somewhat evaporated, shifting back to the original late 1950s and early 1960s approach of males suppressing challenging emotions except anger. I do not believe that anger, sadness, depression, anxiety, guilt, and grief are negative emotions. Instead, these emotions can be understood as challenging feelings we need to learn to identify, accept, and express in healthy ways.

In my twenty-five years of facilitating groups in halfway houses, I have had the privilege of counseling African American, Latine, Asian Pacific, Native American, and Caucasian clients. Individuals may be sent directly to halfway houses or as part of their federal or Colorado Department of Corrections (DOC) sentence. Sometimes, DOC clients strongly associate with their racial and/or ethnic group in prison and become involved in angry rivalries against other incarcerated groups. This, combined with the general anger that clients have for the criminal justice system, plus those involved in the justice system not wanting to appear vulnerable, can create a hostile halfway house environment.

As a licensed professional counselor practicing supportive, empathic CMC integrative counseling, I would often experience a client's anger. Incarceration environments can be very stressful and may trigger staff and client anger. Justice system staff may experience anger at clients for noncompliance, lack of respect, irresponsibility, and rule-breaking behavior. Clients experiencing challenging interactions with justice system staff, loss of privileges, overcrowding, negative living conditions, and exposure to violent situations appear to be at risk for anger-related incidents. As noted previously, CCT and MI suggest criminal justice workers not personalize (take responsibility for) a client's challenging emotions. This is a difficult professional skill to achieve and takes time and patience to develop. It is important for justice system employees to remember clients often displace (project) anger for themselves onto justice system staff.

People in the justice system often struggle with anger, which is exacerbated by their incarceration, parole, or probation restrictions. No one likes being told what to do, especially people involved in the criminal justice system. It has been my experience that people in the justice system are overtold what to do. Those who work directly with clients in the justice system can help them better manage their anger in order to avoid increased consequences. Anger is a challenging emotion. Challenging emotions are not positive or negative, appropriate or inappropriate, and/or healthy or unhealthy. Emotions are feelings that most people experience, and individuals can learn to identify and accept nonjudgmentally by using mindfulness (see below). Some emotions are more challenging to deal with than others.

How people express their anger can be evaluated as healthy or unhealthy, appropriate or inappropriate, and/or positive or negative. Healthy anger

management skills include, yet are not limited to, the time-out technique, rational thinking, and assertive communication. Deep breathing and slow release of breath are immediate anger management skills which can be used alone or in conjunction with these techniques.

It is important for people to be aware of their triggers to better control anger. An anger trigger, similar to an alcohol/drug relapse trigger, is anything that increases one's risk of losing control of their anger. Anger triggers include, yet are not limited to insults, dishonesty, name-calling, cursing, swearing, blaming, ordering, manipulating, finger-pointing, voice-raising, teeth-clenching, and staring. There are low, medium, and high levels of anger that a frustrated individual will benefit from assessing, if possible.

Upon recognizing a trigger and assessing their level of anger, a person involved in the justice system, and/or a criminal justice worker, can implement the most appropriate anger management technique identified above. A criminal justice worker may suggest to a client experiencing anger to use deep breathing and slow release of breath to attempt to calm themselves. A high level of anger indicates the person may best benefit from taking a time-out in order to avoid escalation and a possible violent incident. The angry individual recognizes her/his trigger and proceeds to tell the other person, or people involved, that they are going to take a time-out. A criminal justice worker can also considerately suggest to a client with decreased self-insight that they may benefit from taking a time-out. If possible, a justice system professional might teach a willing client with rage issues about the time-out technique before that person has actually had an anger-related incident. The person taking a time-out walks for 30 minutes (some anger management experts suggest taking a sixty-minute time-out, and it seems essential that a fixed amount of time for the technique is decided upon before it is implemented) and does not use alcohol/drugs or drive. Once they return, they have the option of talking about the issue with the other individual involved if both feel safe, are agreeable and available. This can also be done at a later agreed-upon time.

Most people in the justice system have some access to walking. On the time-out walk, the frustrated individual can think about what is angering them and how to discuss it upon return using direct communication (see Chapter 6, "5. Assertiveness"). The physical activity of walking appears to help an angry person calm down, allowing rational thinking to improve and ultimately the opportunity to discuss the issue peacefully and constructively.

Once an individual is experiencing a moderate to low level of anger, a criminal justice worker might suggest they use rational thinking and assertive direct communication to problem-solve. Honest, respectful, sincere, and genuine communication can help people resolve anger-related issues. *I have observed that the art of in-person empathizing and communicating with others is decreasing. I usually suggest to my clients who are experiencing anger associated with another individual, if they both feel safe doing so, to calmly and genuinely communicate and express their thoughts, emotions, and possible solutions associated with the issue at hand.*

Healthy conflict resolution involves communication with the goal of solving a problem, not winning or losing. Conflict resolution requires listening, being respectful, discussing one issue at a time, and remaining on topic until completion before addressing another problem. If a past unresolved issue arises during the current disagreement, it can be noted and addressed in the future once the issue at hand is resolved. If the issue at hand is a matter of fact, it is each participant's responsibility to have their supportive data. Analyzing the other person, dominating a discussion, interrupting, demanding rather than requesting, name-calling, insulting, raising voices, blaming, not responding to points made or listening to opinions different from one's own, accusing, labeling, and physical force are all destructive to conflict resolution. Often compromising creates a win-win solution that both parties can agree to. Assertiveness (see Chapter 6, "5. Assertiveness") is the behavioral communication skill that can lead to conflict resolution by using therapeutic discussion. Justice system workers can share these skills (the time-out technique, direct communication, and assertiveness) with willing clients in order to help them control, express, and problem-solve their anger-related issues in healthy ways.

8. Victim Impact

Victim impact consideration is a process that helps people involved in the justice system think about how their behavior emotionally, cognitively, psychologically, physically, and financially affected their victims. This information allows people in the justice system to increase their awareness of their victim's experiences and possibly accept greater responsibility for their behavior.[28] Victim impact understanding can help clients develop empathy for their victims and recognize how their behavior affected the injured person's and their own families and communities, and society in general. Victim impact consideration can also help people involved in the justice system understand the trauma associated with victimization and give them another opportunity to think about establishing a prosocial lifestyle. Criminal justice workers can use a caring, factual, and nonjudgmental approach to help clients consider the impacts of their actions on a victim if such a discussion seems timely and appropriate.

9. Mindfulness, Meditation, Positive Thinking, and Gratitude

Criminal justice workers who can suggest and/or model mindfulness, meditation, positive thinking and gratitude can help themselves and those involved in the justice system to be more attentive, calm, open-minded, nonjudgmental, and accepting. Under the topic of psychological suggestion in this chapter, I discussed the evidence-based therapeutic potential of suggestion.

Psychology Today declares "mindfulness is a state of active, open attention (consciousness) to the present. This state is described as observing one's thoughts and feelings without judging them as good or bad." Mindfulness is being in the here and now and observing oneself without being critical.[29] People can be overly self-critical, possibly due to experiencing inadequate beliefs associated with past trauma and/or family of origin issues. If those involved in the justice system can be mindful, self-observing, and curious without overly judging themselves, they may be able to gain increased self-insight which can help them establish a prosocial lifestyle.

The practice of generic meditation, sitting in a comfortable position, eyes closed, focused on a word (mantra) and/or one's slow breath for 5 minutes (a person can start with one minute if five minutes is too uncomfortable and gradually increase their meditation time), and asking thoughts to go away, can help people decrease anxiety, depression, and general stress. Meditation is a method of clearing the mind of thoughts. Meditation, like mindfulness, is a process of self-acceptance that can result in experiencing increased inner peace. This state of calmness can help those involved in the justice system peacefully accept their challenging emotions and more rationally problem-solve difficult issues and situations. A justice system worker might suggest to a willing client that they consider trying meditation in order to attempt to decrease their general depression and anxiety.[30]

Positive thinking is the process of cognitively considering the best possible results of any given situation, no matter what the predicament is. An example of positive thinking is someone involved in the justice system who is depressed about receiving a five-year sentence, recognizing that their incarceration time can significantly decrease if they are compliant with their correctional situation. Generally, many of those involved in the justice system are rewarded for compliant institutional behavior with a shortening of their sentence. Correctional facilities refer to this process as receiving "good time." Positive thinking is essentially evaluating all circumstances with the most optimistic point of view and attitude. The glass is viewed as being half full instead of half empty. Although extremely challenging at times, attitude is something we can consciously control. Justice system workers may help clients gain a more therapeutic attitude and decrease stress by encouraging them to use positive thinking.[31]

Gratitude is the appreciation and thankfulness for what a person has or has experienced. Instead of the often negative human nature of comparing ourselves to others, gratitude involves appreciating what one has or has experienced without comparison. In the United States, social media appears to be a growing aspect of contemporary culture. One disadvantage of social media can be comparing ourselves to others. Often, people experience feelings of inadequacy when comparing their lives to others who might be exaggerating their accomplishments. Comparing our present self to our past self seems to be a healthier way to evaluate progress in our lives rather than equating ourselves to others. Justice system workers assisting clients in recognizing gratitude for what they have and have experienced, and who they are becoming, can support individuals pursuing successful lifestyles.[32]

Evidence-based research supports seven to nine hours of sleep per night, adequate nutrition and diet (including fruits and vegetables), healthy relationships, consistent exercise, caretaking mental health, gratitude, and mindfulness to help people establish and maintain psychological and physical well-being. In our current world of increased stress and anxiety people can unnecessarily activate their fight-or-flight stress response when the situation doesn't call for such. The term emotional dysregulation is often used to describe an individual who is experiencing difficult-to-control feelings that appear to be an overreaction to an observer. A person involved in the justice system may exhibit emotional dysregulation associated with feelings of anger, disappointment, sadness, depression, grief, and anxiety. These intense emotions may trigger impulsive antisocial behaviors, causing a person involved in the justice system significant consequences. A justice system professional knowing this may be able to talk with a willing client who is experiencing a perceived threatening situation and suggest they use mindfulness, meditation, gratitude, and/or positive thinking to decrease anxiety.

If criminal justice workers can be mindful of themselves and those involved in the justice system, they can help themselves psychologically and support clients in pursuing a successful lifestyle. Justice system workers practicing and encouraging willing clients to use mindfulness, meditation, positive thinking and gratitude can aid all involved. These techniques can help justice system professionals and clients be increasingly self-observant, less self-critical, calm, positive, rational, and grateful. Mindfulness, meditation, positive thinking and gratitude techniques can help those involved in the justice system to ultimately establish and maintain a prosocial lifestyle.

10. Parenting

Although I am not a parenting expert, I have helped raise two daughters and read many articles and books about child-rearing. No one likes to be told how to raise their children, and giving unsolicited advice is usually considered inappropriate. One consistent piece of advice I have come across countless times, and wholeheartedly support, is never to discipline children using any kind of physical force, including spanking. The American Psychological Association has taken a stance against physically disciplining children.[33] Many people involved in the justice system often experience anger management issues which, when coupled with the physical discipline of children, can result in criminal child abuse. Justice system workers, when appropriately solicited for advice, can suggest clients use assertive communication, parental modeling (prosocial role modeling), and a decrease in privileges as healthier ways of disciplining children rather than physical punishment. Not only does this advice help a client avoid a possible abuse incident, but these solutions provide a healthy role model for the child and reinforce for the adult nonviolent ways to problem-solve. Violence is never an acceptable solution.

The Process of Transition

People involved in the justice system experience a tremendous amount of change, from freedom to any of the forms of incarceration, and as they transition through the progressive stages of the criminal justice system. Many people find change to be extremely stressful, even when they are making progress. It is important for justice system workers to understand and support clients in the transition process. This will help clients successfully implement the above-stated CBT-oriented techniques and progress through the justice system. *Facilitating transition groups, I often observed new group members being quiet, evaluative, cautious, angry, and resistive. These same clients often ultimately became very active group members. Over my many years of practice, I have observed that building a therapeutic relationship with clients and supporting them in using CMC integrative techniques and skills helped many complete their sentence and establish prosocial lifestyles.* If criminal justice workers can understand the process of transition, they can help clients implement the above-stated CMC techniques and successfully complete their sentence.

Role Modeling

Justice system professionals can be important role models for those under correctional supervision. A role model is defined by Dictionary.com as "a person whose behavior, example, or success serves as a model to be emulated by others, especially by younger people."[34] A role model is a person others want to be like, imitate, look up to, and admire. Justice system professionals and people under correctional supervision oftentimes seem to have similar goals of enjoyable full-time work, the ability to be with friends and/or family after work, independence, and freedom. *At times I have witnessed people involved in the justice system for whom I have facilitated individual and/or group counseling recognizing myself and/or correctional professionals as role models.* Role models can help clients complete their sentences as soon as possible and return to their lives without correctional supervision.

Justice system professionals have the opportunity to be role models given the large amount of time they spend with clients each week. This allows willing staff to display sincere, ethical, honest, reliable, trustworthy, and professional behaviors and values. Justice system professionals who are able and willing to exhibit these values and implement some, if not all, of the above-stated CMC integrative approach techniques can serve as positive role models for clients.

Correctional staff who can model prosocial lifestyles, and support, encourage, teach, mentor, listen to, and build therapeutic relationships with clients can help them in their rehabilitative efforts. Also, justice system workers who choose to define themselves as role models can increase their self-esteem and job satisfaction as this behavior can support clients in establishing and maintaining prosocial lifestyles.

Conclusion

I decided to incorporate CCT, MI, and CBT into the CMC integrative approach because these three psychological methods complement each other in creating a justice system personnel-client healing therapeutic relationship. CCT strongly supports therapeutic relationship-building. MI provides a process for communication about problematic behaviors which an individual may experience ambivalence about changing. CBT interventions contribute skills, techniques, and practices to address the actual problem-solving of clients' issues. *I have discovered that as a psychotherapist, when I combine these psychological approaches, it appears to significantly improve overall client rehabilitation efforts.*

If all justice system workers involved in the police, courts, and corrections can receive information and training in the basics of the CMC integrative approach, they may be able to have a profound therapeutic effect on willing clients. Justice system workers implementing the CMC integrative approach can establish the therapeutic alliance necessary to support clients in creating and maintaining a prosocial lifestyle. Implementing a combination of CCT, MI, and CBT evidence-based skills can provide essential information encouraging clients to establish successful lives. Currently, those working in the justice system usually do not necessarily receive training in these therapies and skills and may be missing an essential opportunity to help willing clients. The more exposure people involved in the justice system are given to the evidence-based, CMC integrative approach, the more likely they may be able to accept their own emotions, use rational thinking, make therapeutic decisions, and implement prosocial behavioral changes. Clients can continue to benefit from CBT individual and/or group therapies including anger management, alcohol/drug recurrence prevention, parenting, transition, domestic violence, DUI, victim impact, and rational thinking.

Justice system workers have an opportunity, and society a responsibility, to significantly increase therapeutic interactions with clients. If justice system employees can gain knowledge of, and implement the CMC integrative approach, clients will receive a significant increase in scientifically proven, therapeutic interactions supporting them in establishing and maintaining successful lifestyles. Not only could the CMC integrative approach expedite clients' rehabilitation, it would also be expected to increase justice system personnel job success and satisfaction, and decrease recidivism.

In my forty years of counseling clients and implemeting the evidence-based CMC integrative approach, I have witnessed more success than the current average. Success rates for people involved in the justice system are low. Improved client rehabilitation results can be measured by expedited criminal sentence completion and reduced recidivism rates. Combining the evidence-based CCT, MI, and CBT therapies to create and implement the CMC integrative approach appears to have a greater potential for client success than current methods employed in the United States' criminal justice system.

7

Putting It All Together

Review, Applications, and Benefits of the CMC Integrative Approach

Every interpersonal interaction that justice system professionals have with clients presents an opportunity to add therapeutically to their rehabilitation process. It would be unrealistic to expect justice system staff to always be conscious of the possibility that each interpersonal interaction they have with clients will be rehabilitation-oriented. That is not the goal of this book. **The goal of this book is to increase awareness that the manner in which justice system staff interact with clients has the potential to contribute to that person's rehabilitation.** If justice system personnel can keep this idea in the forefront of their minds, they have an opportunity to improve rehabilitation for clients and experience an increased sense of success and satisfaction in their work.

The purpose of this chapter is to integrate the general therapeutic concepts, evidence-based knowledge, and healing techniques that comprise the CMC integrative approach. In this chapter, you will also be presented with a comprehensive understanding of how this approach benefits both those involved in the justice system and criminal justice employees. Finally, this chapter will discuss how the CMC integrative approach can benefit the US criminal justice system as well as society in general.

A Psychotherapist's Use of the CMC Integrative Approach

My application of the CMC integrative approach with someone involved in the justice system exhibiting antisocial personality and substance use disorder (SUD) characteristics can illustrate the benefits of this method. Often, a client's therapeutic goals include being the best version of themselves, prosocial, and alcohol/drug sober or using legal substances in a socially responsible manner. These goals can be translated to successful completion of their criminal sentence and maintaining a prosocial lifestyle in the community.

First, I develop a treatment plan with the client to attain their goals, which usually includes cognitive behavioral (CBT) skill-specific group therapy. Using client-centered therapy (CCT), I initially attempt to build a therapeutic alliance, or a healthy professional relationship, through listening, reflecting back what they say to show understanding, being nonjudgmental, and exhibiting empathy. I attempt to recognize the incongruence, or disturbance, the client is experiencing when they evaluate themselves currently (real self) and who they ultimately want to become (ideal self). Through CCT individual and/or group therapy methods, the client has the opportunity to learn about themselves, their past behaviors, and childhood/adult related traumas and gain self-insight. I also take into account any significant sociological, criminological, and/or psychological factors that may be client related. I use my general knowledge of the criminal justice system to empathize with the client's struggles in navigating through the justice system. Most clients will attend cognitive behavioral groups focusing on substance use, rational thinking, and/or prosocial skills in order to learn relapse prevention, anger management, decision-making, and/or socially acceptable problem-solving techniques. Using French and Raven's referent power base, I continue to build a respectful professional relationship with the client throughout this process. This allows the client to continue to trust that I am concerned about them and have their therapeutic goals in mind.

Often, a client will experience ambivalence towards changing antisocial actions to prosocial behaviors. When a client shares their ambivalence, I use motivational interviewing (MI) skills to help them examine their past criminal consequences and future antisocial and prosocial behavior options. I also think about The Stages of Change model and attempt to understand what phase the client is experiencing, discuss it with them, and adjust the treatment plan to use CBT techniques that best meet the client's current needs. I maintain my professional therapeutic commitment to do what is in my client's best interest, usually attempting to help them attain their goals to establish and maintain a sober, prosocial lifestyle. I use patience and persistence to support the client in their efforts to reach their therapeutic goals and address any setbacks that might occur. I receive a signed release of information from all of my clients permitting me to discuss any of their psychological circumstances baffling me with my clinical consultant, who is also one of my mentors. I have found clinical consultation to be a very helpful problem-solving tool when a client is experiencing significant challenges. When implementing the CMC integrative approach method, I have observed improvement in clients' rehabilitation efforts.

Review of Key Concepts from the Previous Chapters

The CMC integrative approach encourages justice system personnel to better understand themselves and clients, the criminal justice system, how people can change, and the evidence-based psychological techniques and processes that can improve rehabilitation.

As discussed in Chapter 1, the CMC integrative approach strongly suggests that justice system employees recognize the **psychological characteristics of clients** and take into account the **sociological factors** that may affect their criminal behavior. The approach also encourages criminal justice system staff to contemplate the evidence-based **criminological** (the study of crime) **considerations** associated with antisocial behavior. Justice system workers are encouraged to think about the racial disparities that exist in the justice system and the adverse childhood experiences (ACEs) clients have encountered in their lives. Understanding the issues people have been subjected to may help workers increase healing **empathy** for clients. It is also important that employees consider the **psychological reactance** clients experience when they perceive that they will, or actually do, lose a behavioral freedom.

As explained in Chapter 2, it is helpful for justice system professionals to **understand the basic concepts of the US criminal justice system** in order to therapeutically empathize with a client's transitions through the system. The police, courts, and corrections make up the three branches of the criminal justice system. Each of these branches is a separate entity and has its unique set of mandates, circumstances, strengths, and deficiencies. These branches come together and overlap at times in an attempt to create smooth transitions for clients.

Chapter 3 discusses **correctional officer (CO) typologies,** or character types, which can help COs and other justice system professionals understand how their personality and experiences affect their interpersonal interactions with clients. It is also important to **recognize the significant employment stressors correctional and police officers encounter** which may result in their experiencing psychological and physical challenges. Justice system personnel in general, and correctional and police officers in particular, can benefit from mental and physical self-care activities.

The CMC integrative approach incorporates **The Transtheoretical Model (TTM)**, better known as **The Stages of Change,** into its framework. When working with people involved in the justice system and using the CMC approach, it can be crucial to recognize a person's level of readiness to make changes. The Transtheoretical Model helps justice system employees better understand how people change an unhealthy action to a healthy behavior. Specifically, COs, and others working in the justice system who are aware of The Transtheoretical Model may be able to support willing clients by defining their specific stage of change and possibly suggesting problem-solving techniques tailored to the particular transitional phase the person is in. Transforming a behavior requires those involved in the justice system to identify their issue, decide to alter their conduct, establish a realistic plan, take action, and ultimately maintain the change.

Chapter 4 discusses **the criminal justice system's employment opportunities, associated qualifications, and the essential value of the mental health training personnel receive.** Training for all justice system staff concerning how to therapeutically interact with clients can be crucial for effective rehabilitation. Training may include a particular focus on effective, evidence-based interactions and mental health interventions that can be implemented with clients. It is very important for justice system professionals, especially correctional, peace, and police officers, to be aware of the mental health education that may be available to them, and the strengths and inadequacies that exist in these training programs. National mandatory accreditation of justice system employee mental health, procedural justice, and empathy training by organizations such as the National Commission on Correctional Health could improve client rehabilitation efforts and decrease recidivism.

In Chapter 5, it was suggested that justice system personnel take into account **French and Raven's personal power bases** and identify which of these influencers they may employ to improve client rehabilitation. Justice system professionals can increase their self-awareness by identifying their own individual personal power base(s) and understanding how these influencers affect client behavior. **The CMC integrative approach encourages justice**

system workers to adopt a therapeutic legitimate, expert and/or referent personal power base and combine it with building a deliberate "therapeutic alliance," or healthy working relationship, with clients. I define this as a "**relationship-building personal power base.**" Scientific evidence supports this to be effective in improving client rehabilitation.

Studies have shown that coercion, an authoritarian power base exhibited by some COs in correctional environments, causes increased future client noncompliance and disobedience. Research has also verified that COs displaying legitimate, expert, and referent power help create safer and more stable correctional environments. Thus, the CMC integrative approach supports COs in attaining two of their essential employment responsibilities: maintaining safe correctional environments and helping to rehabilitate those involved in the justice system.

In Chapter 6, the three evidence-based psychological methods comprising the "**C**" "**M**" "**C**" approach were discussed. These are: Carl Roger's **CCT**, Miller and Rollnick's **MI**, and Beck's **CBT.** CCT, MI, and CBT all emphasize the importance of the therapeutic alliance: the healthy, ethical, professional, and psychological healing relationship between the justice system employee and client. CCT encourages self-insight and behavior change as clients pursue becoming the best versions of themselves. MI helps ambivalent clients make successful decisions and promotes prosocial behavior. CBT encourages individuals to change irrational thoughts and actions to rational beliefs and behaviors. Often, when clients recognize and change irrational beliefs to rational thoughts, they decrease associated challenging emotions, which may include depression, anxiety, guilt, and sadness. CBT techniques can help those involved in the justice system change antisocial actions to prosocial behaviors. **CCT, MI, and CBT combined support prosocial behavior and have the potential to expedite and improve client rehabilitation.**

Chapter 6 also discusses how justice system workers can employ the CMC integrative approach and its scientifically proven CBT techniques to aid in

client rehabilitation. Justice system personnel employing the psychological techniques of suggestion, rational thinking, problem-solving, assertiveness, meditation, positive thinking, mindfulness, and gratitude can help improve client rehabilitation. Justice system professionals who understand alcohol/drug relapse prevention, anger management, victim impact, parenting, and the steps of transition can help willing clients recognize and successfully navigate associated challenging processes. Finally, criminal justice workers have an opportunity to role model a prosocial lifestyle for those involved in the justice system.

In summary, the CMC integrative approach promotes the belief that every interpersonal interaction that justice system professionals have with a client has the potential to help in their rehabilitation process. If justice system workers are better able to psychologically understand themselves and clients, they may be able to improve their therapeutic alliance efforts and increase empathy for those involved in the justice system. A justice system worker's knowledge of the criminal justice system, how people change, their personal power base(s), CCT, MI, CBT and associated techniques can aid client rehabilitation. The CMC integrative approach encourages justice system professionals to incorporate this information to create a therapeutic relationship-building personal power base with clients in order to expedite and improve rehabilitation efforts.

The Benefits of the CMC Integrative Approach for Those Involved in the Justice System

The CMC integrative approach can greatly benefit those involved in the justice system. Although much of the research described throughout this book supports how the various components of the approach can benefit clients, it is important to consolidate the many features of this method to make the information easily accessible. Doing so will give the reader a condensed psychological perspective of an approach that can decrease recidivism.

The CMC integrative approach combines three evidence-based treatment modalities, and aspects of each of these methods can be used by justice system workers when interacting with clients. In a broader sense, the approach's foundation is built on the justice system employee creating a professional and empathic therapeutic relationship with a client.

COs understanding their own typology, or character type, as defined by researchers King and Labrecque in a 2017 study, and French and Raven's referent, expert, and legitimate personal power base(s) can develop improved therapeutic interactions with individuals. These concepts can contribute to therapeutic relationship-building and rehabilitation for those involved in the justice system.

Those involved in the justice system can benefit from staff implementing the CMC integrative approach. The approach suggests staff use **empathy, the therapeutic alliance**, healthy **relationship-building practices, CCT** methods, **MI** strategies, and **CBT** techniques.

Empathy, the capacity to think and feel the thoughts and emotions of others, greatly benefits those involved in the justice system. The three primary modalities comprising the CMC integrative approach and the research reviewed in prior chapters consistently stress the key significance of building an empathic relationship. When justice system personnel display empathy, clients are more likely to believe that they are recognized, listened to, understood, respected, and appreciated. This empathic interaction can support those involved in the justice system's individual efforts to rehabilitate themselves.

In a 2021 study titled "A Scalable Empathic Supervision Intervention to Mitigate Recidivism From Probation and Parole," researchers found that clients of probation and parole officers who received empathy training experienced a 13 percent decrease in recidivism. The researchers surveyed

216 parole and probation officers who, after receiving empathy training, also recognized an increased emotional connection to their clients.[1] This study illustrates the need for justice system personnel empathy training, and how empathic relationship-building interactions between staff and clients can decrease recidivism, a relapse into criminal behavior. *I have facilitated SUD counseling for thousands involved in the justice system. There remain many people who believe SUD is a choice, which appears to blame clients. Medical evidence suggests SUDs are caused by genetic and environmental factors contributing to a person's unquenchable desire for alcohol/drugs. I use the empathic medical approach with SUD clients, which appears to support client rehabilitation.*

Similarly, **the therapeutic alliance** is a mutually beneficial working relationship between the justice system employee and client. A 2019 literature review of pertinent research titled "Mandated Treatment and Its Impact on Therapeutic Process and Outcome Factors," authored by Henning Hachtel, Tobias Vogel, and Christian G. Huber, found that recidivism can be reduced if treatment focuses on maintaining a meaningful professional justice system worker–client relationship, is evidence-based, and caring.[2]

In general, professional, ethical, **healthy relationship-building practices** can help those involved in the justice system with their rehabilitation efforts. Therapeutic communication, trust, listening, respect, assertiveness, boundaries, appreciation, honesty, accepting disagreements, and being responsible are all important elements of creating and maintaining a mutually respectful, healthy relationship. By role modeling professional relationship-building techniques for clients, justice system staff can help them improve their interpersonal and prosocial skills. Learning and ultimately implementing relationship-building skills can help clients create healthy interpersonal interactions with others.

Justice system personnel and clients may benefit from communicating assertively with each other in order to achieve their respective corrections and treatment goals. Justice system workers are usually attempting to maintain a safe correctional facility while clients are striving to progress through the criminal justice system. Assertiveness techniques include asking for what a person wants while taking into serious consideration the other individual's thoughts and feelings. Justice system employees and clients can use assertiveness techniques to build trust, which can result in them being more reliable and dependable, doing what they say they will do. Careful listening, being honest, and requesting fairness are assertive relationship-building practices. Assertiveness also involves attempting to resolve conflicts using therapeutic confrontation in which feelings, thoughts, and solutions are peacefully discussed. The CMC integrative approach benefits clients by teaching and supporting problem-solving assertive communication techniques that can aid in their rehabilitation.

When justice system workers and clients implement healthy relationship-building practices and techniques, they create an opportunity to increase their general trust for one another. When a challenging therapeutic confrontation between a justice system worker and a client occurs, it is this trust that may allow healthy limit setting, the establishment of boundaries, and possible therapeutic consequences. This may permit justice system employees and clients to be more likely to accept disagreements and possible consequences that could result from a challenging incident. The use of professional relationship-building practices by justice system workers can ultimately help clients build trust and learn from therapeutic consequences.

CCT is one of the three essential therapeutic methods that make up the CMC integrative approach. CCT promotes the idea that clients are experts on their own lives and encourages justice system workers to respect them. CCT also emphasizes the concept that clients are striving to become the best version of themselves and supports staff giving them the benefit of the doubt.

CCT helps those involved in the justice system to increase therapeutic self-awareness, knowledge of one's own thoughts, feelings, and behaviors, and how these affect themselves and others. CCT encourages clients to therapeutically express challenging emotions that may emerge from their experiences with the justice system. Although such displays of emotions may be taxing for justice system workers to hear, it is important for employees not to take this type of expression personally and to recognize when clients are learning to gain self-insight and an ability to appropriately and safely verbalize their emotions. Permitting this process to unfold may help clients learn to label and express their emotions in a more regulated, calm manner. As those involved in the justice system gain a better understanding of how come they behave in a certain manner, the consequences of their actions, and their behavioral options, they may develop increased motivation to choose prosocial behaviors. This client self-awareness, combined with the CCT concept that all people are a part of humanity, may help clients and justice system personnel work together to problem-solve issues.

MI is the second therapeutic method that makes up the CMC integrative approach. MI techniques can assist clients in overcoming ambivalence. Rather than directly confronting clients, justice system staff using MI are encouraged to be empathic, listen to a client's dissatisfaction with their current circumstances, and point out the discrepancies between their goals and past antisocial behaviors. To accomplish this effectively, justice system staff can identify the client's readiness to change (see Chapter 3, "The Stages of Change"). This interaction between justice system workers and clients can help the latter evaluate the consequences of their past antisocial actions, contemplate conduct options, resolve ambivalence, and eventually make a commitment to prosocial behavioral change. MI encourages clients to use CBT techniques such as rational thinking, problem-solving, and alcohol/drug relapse/recurrence prevention. Implementing these techniques may help clients solidify their commitment to prosocial behavioral changes. MI is an evidence-based approach that has been demonstrated to effectively treat SUDs[3] and reduce recidivism.[4]

CBT is the third therapeutic method that makes up the CMC integrative approach. CBT promotes the concept that problematic behaviors and emotional overreactions may be the result of irrational thinking. CBT encourages clients to identify, reevaluate, and replace cognitive distortions with rational thoughts and behaviors. CBT also suggests that when clients can change their irrational thinking and associated behaviors, they may be able to decrease the intensity of related challenging emotions. Those involved in the justice system can benefit from CBT by learning and implementing thought and behavior techniques to help them manage and change cognitive distortions, challenging emotions, and antisocial behaviors.

The expanding field of CBT interventions includes a wide range of techniques and practices in areas such as rational thinking, decision-making, problem-solving, assertiveness, alcohol/drug relapse prevention, anger management, victim impact, mindfulness, positive thinking, gratitude, and parenting skills. CBT is consistent with the spirit of the CMC integrative approach in that it does not support telling individuals what to do. Instead, CBT encourages justice system workers to generate discussion, ask questions, and share information with clients in order to create a mutually respectful and collaborative therapeutic working relationship. CBT research indicates that CBT approaches have been very effective in reducing recidivism.[5]

In summary, the CMC integrative approach combines evidence-based therapy processes and techniques that have been found to enhance rehabilitation and decrease recidivism. The CMC approach stresses the importance of an empathic therapeutic alliance and healthy relationship-building practices and integrates CCT methods, MI strategies, and CBT techniques. This approach provides an opportunity for those involved in the justice system to gain self-insight, engage in successful rehabilitation processes, establish a prosocial lifestyle, and reduce their chances of recidivating.

The Benefits of the CMC Integrative Approach for Justice System Personnel

Implementing CMC integrative approach methods for clients can have many benefits for justice system personnel. Justice system employees incorporating this approach into their daily responsibilities can improve job success and satisfaction through decreasing client recidivism, enhancing rehabilitation, creating safer correctional facilities, and improving community relations. In addition, staff may also obtain personal benefits including increased self-awareness, empathy, therapeutic relationships with clients, and enhancing their own well-being.

In a June 2023 research review, the authors found that therapeutic interventions offered in a variety of ways for incarcerated individuals had the potential to improve work satisfaction for justice system employees.[6] COs implementing therapeutic techniques with clients can experience a sense of satisfaction, achievement, and purpose.

Justice system personnel who choose to implement CMC integrative approach methods can expect clients to be more successful in pursuing their goal of establishing a prosocial lifestyle. Witnessing these successes can improve staff satisfaction. *The motivation to write this book stemmed from my twenty-five years of facilitating halfway house counseling using the CMC approach and a sense of purpose related to improving the justice system.*

Justice system personnel, especially COs, can receive physical and mental health benefits from using CMC integrative approach methods to maintain safer incarceration facilities. Steiner and Wooldredge's 2018 research review indicated that in most cases COs exhibiting French and Raven's legitimate, referent, and/or expert personal power bases in prisons resulted in decreased client rule-breaking behavior, very possibly creating safer incarceration environments (see Chapter 5). It would be expected that safer incarceration environments would decrease justice system personnel workplace anxiety and risk for physical injury.

COs consistently using empathy, therapeutic alliance-like relationship-building skills, listening, and CBT techniques have an opportunity to help create a healthier correctional facility environment. This type of correctional therapeutic community may make it easier for COs to deescalate potentially dangerous situations. In an October 2021 study titled "The Role of Prison Officers' Regulation of Inmates Affect on Their Exposure to Violent Behaviors and the Development of PTSD Symptoms," author David Martinez-Inigo found that COs implementing emotional regulation therapeutic techniques (e.g., deep breathing; fact checking, which is a form of rational thinking) with clients in order to decrease their level of anger, fear, and/or other challenging emotions reduced the likelihood of a client's exhibiting violent behavior. This study was based on the results of a questionnaire completed by 424 prison officers employed at five Uruguayan prisons.[7] Thus, COs implementing therapeutic interventions consistent with the CMC integrative approach would be expected to reduce correctional facility violence and improve staff physical safety and mental health.

When justice system personnel learn and implement CMC integrative approach methods, they are also likely to gain increased self-awareness. Self-awareness can be understood as a person's potential to identify and interpret their feelings, thoughts, and behaviors, and understand how they affect other people. It can be natural for people to relate newly learned psychological information and approaches directly to their own lives and gain increased self-awareness and understanding by doing so.

Justice system workers may find that increased self-awareness can improve their lives. In a 2022 article titled "The Benefits of Self-Awareness," author Shelley Aronov-Jacoby, a clinical social worker, states that self-awareness offers many rewards including improved emotional control, communication, decision-making, relationships, happiness, confidence, work satisfaction, leadership skills, and overall perspective.[8] Justice system employees using the CMC integrative approach may increase their self-awareness and, in doing so, enhance their general well-being.

Justice system staff implementing the CMC integrative approach may also achieve personal benefits from the use of empathy. Justice system personnel who implement CMC integrative approach methods will learn a significant amount about empathy, which is a central theme of the therapeutic alliance, CCT, MI, and CBT. In an article titled "Why It's OK to Be Empathic Toward Inmates," Anthony Gangi, an over 20-year veteran of corrections and an Associate Administrator for State Corrections (New Jersey) at the time of this writing, strongly supports correction system staff using empathy as a general problem-solving technique in correctional facilities.[9] Similarly, research cited throughout this book supports that the use of empathy can help justice system workers build therapeutic relationships with clients, deescalate violent incarceration incidents, maintain safer correctional facilities, and decrease recidivism.

In summary, the CMC integrative approach can be beneficial for justice system personnel individually and to the wider community. Individually, the approach provides a framework to engage in beneficial professional therapeutic relationship-building with clients. By engaging in constructive relationship-building, COs can benefit from gaining self-insight, decreasing the risk of negative client interactions, and increasing job satisfaction.[10]

As it relates to the community, justice system staff implementing the CMC integrative approach can help create safer correctional facilities, improve client rehabilitation, and enhance community relations. The essential interaction between justice system personnel and the community will be elaborated on in the next section of this chapter when the concept of "procedural justice," discussed in Chapter 4, is reviewed. The CMC integrated approach includes "procedural justice," the community's belief that the criminal justice system is fair because it treats society with dignity and respect. Procedural justice benefits justice system staff, the community, and the criminal justice system.

Overall, implementing CMC integrative approach methods can enhance justice system personnel's physical and psychological well-being and community relations.

The Benefits of the CMC Integrative Approach for the US Criminal Justice System and Society

Implementing the CMC integrative approach has the potential to benefit the United States's criminal justice system and society. These benefits include reducing recidivism, improving public safety, decreasing the costs of incarceration, curtailing crime, addressing an individual's underlying psychological issues associated with criminal behavior (mental health, substance use, trauma, irrational thinking, and/or inadequate problem-solving skills), and allowing for more effective client rehabilitation and reintegration back into society. Also, CMC methods benefit the criminal justice system and society by encouraging procedural justice opportunities. The criminal justice system can benefit from CMC methods by becoming a more successful therapeutic resource for those involved in the justice system. Society can benefit by spending fewer taxpayer dollars for justice system expenses and by having people involved in the justice system return to become contributing, prosocial members of the community.

As previously discussed, evidence-based studies have indicated that therapeutic techniques associated with CBT reduce client recidivism.[11]

Reducing recidivism can help to 1) improve public and community safety by decreasing possible future crime rates and arrests; 2) lower taxpayer costs due to the decreased number of future incarcerated individuals; and 3) support the rehabilitation of those involved in the justice system to become contributing community members.[12, 13]

CMC integrative approach therapeutic interventions can improve public safety by helping clients reintegrate into society and establish a prosocial lifestyle. In a 2021 research article, titled "A Better Path Forward for Criminal Justice: Changing Prisons to Help People Change," authors Christy Visher and John Eason, associated with the Brookings-AEI Working Group on Criminal Justice Reform, conclude that prison environments are crucial to community public health and safety. The authors state that those involved in the justice system struggle to reintegrate into communities because the environment in most prisons is not conducive to therapeutic change. Visher and Eason go on to suggest that implementing evidence-based therapeutic interventions, like CBT, in correctional facilities will help those involved in the justice system establish prosocial lifestyles in their communities.[14] Clients who take advantage of their opportunities to engage in justice system therapeutic interventions, complete their criminal sentence, and reenter their communities would be expected to have a greater probability of not committing crimes in the future and establishing a prosocial lifestyle.

Before examining the cost-effectiveness of imprisonment in the United States, it is important to understand who actually pays the costs of incarceration. In an article titled "Economics of Incarceration: The Economic Drivers and Consequences of Mass Incarceration," the Prison Policy Initiative, a nonprofit criminal justice think tank based in Massachusetts, has consolidated much of the research concerning economic factors associated with incarceration in the United States. According to the Prison Policy Initiative, federal, state, and local government taxes, and sometimes those involved in the justice system themselves, pay for the costs of incarceration.[15] A taxpayer in the United States is usually a business or an individual that is required to pay federal, state, and local government taxes. In a 2012 study titled "Price of Prisons: What Incarceration Costs Taxpayers," Christian Hendrickson and Ruth Delaney, using a methodology for calculating the cost of prisons to taxpayers, found that individual taxpayers pay the majority of costs for people who are incarcerated.[16]

Cost-effectiveness of mental health treatment in the US justice system appears to be one important financial issue that affects taxpayers. Although research seems to be limited, studies indicate that mental health treatment in incarceration facilities appears to be cost-effective, benefiting the criminal justice system and society. In a 2023 literature review titled "Economic

Evaluations of Mental Health Interventions in Criminal Justice," authors Martin Knapp and Gloria Wong found that, although there are not many high-quality studies related to this topic, there was evidence that psychological interventions for individuals who are incarcerated are cost-effective. Specifically, the authors state that CBT and therapeutic communities are cost-effective.[17]

The CMC integrative approach includes CBT, which has been found to be effective in reducing crime. Thus, clients who engage in CBT justice system treatment would probably be less likely to commit a future crime. Similarly, in a 2010 National Institute of Justice (NIJ) article titled "Preventing Future Crime With Cognitive Behavioral Therapy," author Patrick Clark states that CBT reduces recidivism and is effective in justice system institutions and the community (i.e., parole and probation).[18] The CMC integrative approach benefits society and the justice system by reducing crime.

The CMC integrative approach can help clients address their underlying psychological issues associated with criminal behavior. Although the CMC integrative approach does not suggest justice system personnel act as clients' psychotherapists, it does promote staff interacting with individuals in a therapeutic manner. Justice system psychotherapists can facilitate individual and/or group counseling to help willing clients process underlying psychological issues associated with their antisocial behavior. However, **the contribution of all levels of justice system staff is of crucial importance to reinforce client progress.** Justice system personnel can learn to apply many of the healing CMC integrative approach techniques. Staff may be better able to interact therapeutically as they become more aware of the psychological issues clients may be facing. These issues can include ASPD and/or SUD characteristics, trauma associated with ACEs and incarceration, and mental health issues often associated with anxiety and depression.

According to an information website established by the National Alliance on Mental Illness (NAMI) and titled "Mental Health Treatment While Incarcerated," individuals experiencing psychological challenges may have significant difficulty managing the stressors of jail or prison. Those involved in the justice system who experience serious psychological challenges may exhibit behaviors in jail/prison that are not commonly handled through usual correctional facility operations. This may result in these clients being given consequences, like solitary confinement and/or loss of visitation privileges, that could be detrimental to their already existing mental health struggles. Increased and improved mental health treatment in correctional facilities could be one factor leading to more successful results for clients for whom the usual rules of the system may be counterproductive. Thus, there seems to be a significant need for using approaches that address the wide range of mental health issues that may occur in correctional facilities.[19] Therapeutic CMC techniques can help improve the general mental health of clients with psychological challenges and justice system rehabilitation rates, benefiting the justice system and society.

The previous information in this section illustrates that CMC integrative approach methods implemented with those involved in the justice system can benefit society, the criminal justice system, and clients by helping them attain their rehabilitation and community reintegration goals. Through effective rehabilitation, clients may be more likely to establish a productive prosocial lifestyle in their community. Clients who receive and learn therapeutic interventions in correctional facilities and complete their sentence can return to their community and have an opportunity to implement their newly learned thinking and behavioral skills. Such CBT skills, including rational thinking, alcohol/drug relapse (recurrence) prevention, anger management, decision-making, problem-solving, and assertiveness, can support clients with their successful reintegration into society.

The CMC integrative approach therapeutically promotes "procedural justice" practices which also benefit the criminal justice system and society. The concept of procedural justice involves how the community views criminal justice system practices, with the goal being that society evaluates it as operating in a fair manner. By applying CMC integrative approach methods, the justice system can be viewed by the community as promoting procedural justice. In Chapter 4, procedural justice was described as the manner in which police and other authorities communicate with civilians, and how the characteristics of these interactions influence 1) the public's opinion of these authorities; 2) law abidance; and 3) crime rates. **A primary procedural justice goal is for the criminal justice system to build trust with communities.** One way for authorities to build trust with communities is to display empathy. If police are viewed by society as exhibiting empathy, they can advance procedural justice goals and be viewed more favorably by clients and the community.

Research has confirmed that when police consistently employ procedural justice practices, crime can be reduced. Procedural justice methods benefit the criminal justice system by increasing client success rates, reducing arrests and crime, and improving the public's opinion of law enforcement officers. Procedural justice processes can benefit society by reducing community arrests, incarceration, and associated costs. It appears that when community members believe they are being treated fairly, with respect, and listened to by the police and/or other authorities, they are more likely to follow the laws, cooperate with police, and build a more stable community.

A positive relationship between the criminal justice system and communities can also connect civilians to justice system resources. A 2022 study mentioned in Chapter 4, titled "Reforming the Police Through Procedural Justice Training: A Multicity Randomized Trial at Crime Hot Spots," indicated that procedural justice officer training is beneficial to police, civilians, and possibly those involved in the justice system. Procedural justice supports peace officers being trustworthy, neutral, impartial, and transparent in law enforcement decision-making. Research has shown that procedural justice techniques implemented by the police increase 1) their fair behavioral practices with civilians; 2) citizens having a more positive opinion of peace officers; and 3) crime prevention.[20] Procedural justice techniques can also benefit justice system personnel by increasing community support for the criminal justice system in general, and peace officers in particular. When properly implemented, these methods can result in building a healthier relationship with the community, and the community viewing the justice system as a more trusted and valuable resource.

Conclusion

Implementation of the CMC integrative approach can yield many benefits for clients, justice system personnel, the criminal justice system, and society. A wide range of research has been cited indicating that those involved in the justice system who receive effective therapeutic interventions are less likely to engage in future criminal behaviors and more likely to be rehabilitated and successfully reintegrate into their communities. To achieve maximum success, therapeutic interventions would ideally be performed consistently by all levels of justice system staff and occur in a wide variety of situations. Justice system workers can benefit from implementing therapeutic interventions with clients, leading to safer correctional facilities, increased client success, and greater job satisfaction. The United States's criminal justice system benefits from the CMC integrative approach through increased client success rates and the creation of a more beneficial corrections system resource for the community. Communities that witness those who were involved in the justice system becoming successful society members may increasingly view the criminal justice system as a rehabilitative resource. Society can benefit through decreased taxpayer spending for incarceration and the return of rehabilitated clients to their communities. Successful implementation of CMC integrative methods by justice system personnel can further procedural justice goals by increasing community trust in law enforcement and encouraging a more favorable view of the justice system as a supportive resource.

Clients, justice system personnel, the criminal justice system, and society may all benefit significantly from the implementation of the CMC integrative approach. Each of these entities has an opportunity and a responsibility to implement optimal therapeutic interventions with clients. All of these entities can be viewed as interwoven in the goals of reducing crime and recidivism and improving client rehabilitation. The multiple components that make up the CMC integrative approach have been supported by a wide range of research, and it has significant potential to further the goals of mental health criminal justice reform and improved client rehabilitation.

8

The CMC Integrative Approach

A Positive Step for US Criminal Justice Reform

Criminal justice reform is defined by the National Committee for Responsive Philanthropy (NCRP), a Washington, D.C.-based watchdog group promoting the welfare of social justice movements, as a very broad term that refers to any efforts to improve the criminal justice system. The NCRP's definition of the criminal justice system includes the police, prosecution, the court system, corrections, and client reintegration into their community.[1] In general, efforts toward justice system reform support making the lives of individuals involved in the justice system physically safer, healthier, and more rehabilitative. Criminal justice reform in the United States includes a wide variety of issues such as mass incarceration, racial inequities in sentencing, juvenile justice, solitary confinement, police brutality, prison conditions, voting rights, the death penalty, rehabilitation, drug policy reform, and health/dental care in prison. Finally, and particularly relevant to this book, criminal justice reform can also include improved and expanded therapeutic interventions and mental health treatment for justice system clients. The CMC integrative approach, understood as a psychological method and associated therapeutic interventions for those involved in the justice system, can be seen as an essential part of criminal justice reform in the United States.

Some Notable Events in the History of Criminal Justice System Reform

The US criminal justice reform movement has a lengthy history highlighted by some significant legal, social, and political events. The following are only some of the noteworthy justice system reform-related events that have occurred over the last one hundred years.

The US criminal justice prison reform movement may be recognized as beginning in the late 1800s and continuing to the present. A historical review by Study.com, an online learning platform, describes the Prison Reform Movement from the late 1800s to the early 1900s as part of the Progressive Era, an increased industrialization period that occurred in the United States. The Progressive Era initiated the implementation of parole and probation processes, which were an important prison reform issue from 1930 to 1970.[2]

In 1971, President Nixon initiated the "War on Drugs," leading to proposed government actions to decrease drug trafficking and use. The "War on Drugs" continued with President Reagan's Anti-Drug Abuse Acts of 1986 and 1988, which disproportionately affected African Americans, Indigenous, Latine, Asian, and other people of color. Also, in the late 1980s, several prominent politicians advocated for the decriminalization of drugs.

In 1991, Rodney King, an African American man, was severely beaten in Los Angeles, California, by white police officers, motivating widespread calls for criminal justice reform with regard to police brutality, including members of the Congressional Black Caucus Foundation (CBC). The CBC, made up of African American members of the US Congress, is an educational foundation that researches issues affecting African Americans, produces a yearly report on associated legislation, sponsors educational opportunities, and can be viewed as a criminal justice reform group. The CBC has continued to develop specific task forces, including criminal justice reform efforts, to address equal access to resources that improve the quality of all people's lives.[3]

In 2008, President George W. Bush signed "The Second Chance Act," a law providing federal grant money to government agencies and nonprofit organizations to assist in client community reintegration services. "The Second Chance Act" supported housing, substance use disorder treatment, education, and employment training and assistance for those involved in the justice system, with the goal of reducing recidivism and improving community safety. "The Second Chance Act" was supported by leaders in the police, court, corrections, and mental health sectors.[4]

In 2020, George Floyd, an African American, was murdered in Minneapolis, Minnesota, by a white police officer. His murder ignited a mass movement protesting the criminal justice system's racial injustices and discrimination against African Americans, Indigenous, Latine, Asian, and other people of color. George Floyd's death initiated renewed calls for criminal justice reform.[5]

Addressing Mental Health as a Step Toward Criminal Justice Reform

Evidence-based therapeutic interventions, which have been found to benefit people involved in the justice system and reduce recidivism, can present enormous potential for ongoing criminal justice reform. The psychotherapy methods discussed throughout this book that comprise the CMC integrative approach enable justice system staff to understand and therapeutically address the mental health, substance use, and trauma-related issues that contribute to a client's antisocial behavior.

In particular, cognitive behavioral therapy (CBT), which has been widely applied in the criminal justice system, includes teaching evidence-based techniques, skills, and/or practices that can be very helpful for clients.[6] CBT suggests that irrational thoughts and associated learned inadequate behaviors cause clients to experience psychological issues. CBT interventions can result in a client being more likely to learn therapeutic coping skills and exhibit prosocial behaviors. Application of CBT interventions, techniques, and practices can improve individual mental health and benefit the criminal justice system by advancing rehabilitation and reform efforts.

As discussed in previous chapters, client-centered therapy (CCT) can be applied in the justice system to support an individual's motivation to self-actualize and be the best version of themselves. Through self-actualizing, clients can improve their self-concept, and in turn, progress toward changing antisocial actions to prosocial behaviors.

Motivational interviewing (MI) is the third counseling approach discussed in this book that can be implemented by justice system personnel to support rehabilitation and reform efforts. By gradually confronting their ambivalence about change, clients can develop a capacity to decide if prosocial behavior options might yield better results for them in the future. Research has confirmed that MI is an effective counseling approach[7] and can bolster justice system reform efforts.

Evidence-based CBT, CCT, and MI all encourage justice system personnel to use empathy and alliance techniques to build therapeutic relationships with clients. Clients can also benefit from justice system staff modeling prosocial behaviors. Through the use of empathy, role modeling, relationship-building, and CBT techniques justice system personnel can build healing, problem-solving oriented relationships with clients that can aid in their rehabilitation.

If the entire range of justice system personnel can become familiar with the CMC evidence-based therapeutic approaches and interventions discussed in this book, they can implement skills, techniques, and practices that can help clients maintain prosocial lifestyles. The CMC integrative approach has the potential to become a valuable step in mental health criminal justice system reform.

The Spirit of the CMC Integrative Approach

Throughout the discussion of the CMC integrative approach, it has been examined at the specific level, combining CCT, MI, and CBT methods, as well as at a broader level which includes a variety of interactive skills, techniques, practices, and interventions. Together, these specific therapies and broader interventions can be viewed as having a common spirit. **The overriding spirit of the CMC approach calls for using collaboration, empathy, and respect to build therapeutic relationships.** Over and above the value of combining CCT, MI, and CBT, the spirit of the CMC integrative approach can be viewed as the key ingredient of this method. The spirit and implementation of the CMC integrative approach can result in improved client rehabilitation and employee success and satisfaction. The CMC integrative approach can be a significant step in justice system reform.

The spirit of the CMC integrative approach also advocates that justice system personnel understand the basic working processes of the US criminal justice system in order to benefit clients and themselves. When justice system personnel have knowledge about how the police, courts, and corrections interplay, they can increase their empathy for clients who are usually required to navigate the many complexities of this system. This understanding can support those involved in the justice system with their rehabilitation efforts and improve client success rates.

Justice system personnel can further support clients by increasing their understanding of how behavioral sciences factor into rehabilitation. Justice system staff can become more therapeutically effective with clients by recognizing the psychological, sociological, and criminological factors associated with antisocial behavior. This understanding includes an awareness of a client's adverse childhood experiences (ACEs) and the psychological reactance associated with losing behavioral freedoms. Also, justice system workers aware of The Stages of Change, how clients transform antisocial actions to prosocial behaviors, can aid rehabilitation attempts.

The spirit of the CMC integrative approach also supports the concept of justice system personnel improving their self-awareness and self-care in order to aid in client rehabilitation and decrease employment stressors. Justice system staff who can increase their awareness of their worker typology (character type) and use of French and Raven's personal power base(s) can apply this knowledge to improve their therapeutic alliance with clients. The opportunity for justice system personnel to engage in available mental health training can help them therapeutically interact with clients experiencing psychological challenges. Client mental health training can also benefit justice system personnel by increasing their own self-awareness and self-care, as newly learned psychological information is often applied to oneself. It is essential for justice system personnel to engage in self-care behavior in order to deal with their extremely stressful employment processes. The spirit of the CMC integrative approach supports improved client rehabilitation and justice system staff self-care.

Conclusion

The CMC integrative approach can be understood as a psychological method that incorporates evidence-based therapies and interventions, including skills, techniques, and practices. The CMC method is not in itself a new psychological theory and/or intervention. It combines three widely used evidence-based methods: CCT, MI, and CBT. This combination involves, and is enhanced by, the spirit of CMC, emphasizing a collaborative, respectful, empathic, and healing justice system personnel-client therapeutic relationship. Implementation of this approach incorporates the use of evidence-based interventions that can be facilitated by knowledgeable, and increasingly self-aware justice system personnel.

The main thesis of this book is that widespread implementation of the combined components of the CMC integrative approach could lead to more effective and improved client rehabilitation in the US criminal justice system. The CMC integrative approach has the potential to be a crucial next step in mental health criminal justice reform and improve the overall functioning and success of the justice system.

ACKNOWLEDGMENTS

I am grateful to the many people who were instrumental in helping me write this book. My initial thanks go to the women and men involved in the justice system who taught me so much and inspired me to attempt to improve their incarceration, parole, and probation experiences. Also, thank you to the many criminal justice personnel I have worked with over twenty-five years who supported reform efforts. I am grateful that Becca Beurer, Senior Acquisitions Editor at Bloomsbury Publishing, provided me the opportunity to pursue writing this book. Thank you to Sarah E. Rinehart, Assistant Acquisitions Editor, Melissa McClellan, Production Editor, and Bailey Ross, Editorial Assistant at Bloomsbury Publishing for their editing help. Thank you to Vlad Mateescu, Project Manager at Deanta for his production management. Thank you to David Cutler and Adam Brickner for their justice system support. I also thank Laura Temin, Frank Haurwitz, Richard Spiegle, and Lizzy Schweber for their psychological and genuine encouragement. Joseph Fanganello provided me with legal assistance for which I am grateful. I truly appreciated Joe Vellella's significant indexing support. Thank you to Megan Duffy for inspiring me to write, and for helping with editing. Francis Hartogh and Katie Schweber also aided me in editing, for which I am grateful. Finally, a huge thank you to Kathy Sacks and Susan Richstone who assisted in editing this book.

NOTES

Introduction

1 Anderson, R. (2019). One in 55 Adults on Probation or Parole, Study Finds. *Prison Legal News*, 61.

2 Merriam-Webster. (n.d.). In Merriam-Webster.com Dictionary. Retrieved January 14, 2025 from https://www.merriam-webster.com/dictionary.

Chapter 1

1 U.S. Department of Justice. (2024, May 30). About 2% of Adult U.S. Residents Under Correctional Supervision in 2022 [Press Release]. Retrieved January 23, 2024 from https://ojp.gov/archives/pressreleases/2024/about-2-percent-adult-us-residents-under-correctional-supervision-2022.

2 Buehler, E., and Kluckow, R. (2024, May 30). Correctional Populations in the United States, 2022-Statistical Tables. *U.S. Department of Justice. Bureau of Justice Statistics.* https://bjs.ojp.gov/library/publications/correctional-populations-united-states-2022-statistical-tables.

3 Gramlich, J. (2024, April 24). What the Data Says About Crime in the U.S. *Pew Research.* https://www.pewresearch.org/short-reads/2024/04/24/what-the-data-says-about-crime-in-the-us/.

4 Federal Bureau of Investigation. (2024, September 23). FBI Releases 2023 Crime in the Nation Statistics [Press Release]. https://www.fbi.gov/news/press-releases/fbi-releases-2023-crime-in-the-nation-statistics.

5 United States Federal Bureau of Investigation. (n.d.). Crime in the United States 2018. *FBI-UCR Program.* Retrieved July 14, 2023 from https://ucr.fbi.gov/crime-in-the-u.s/2018/crime-in-the-u.s.-2018/topic-pages/violent-crime.

6 Statista. (2023, October 20). Reported Violent Crime Rate in the U.S. from 1990–2022. *Statista.* https://www.statista.com/statistics/191219/reported-violent-crime-rate-in-the-usa-since-1990/.

7 American Psychiatric Association. (2022). *Diagnostic and Statistical Manual of Mental Disorders* (5th ed., text rev.).

8 See Note #7.

9 Califano, Jr., J.A. (2010, February). Behind Bars II: Substance Abuse and America's Prison Population. *National Ctr on Addiction and Substance Abuse at Columbia University (CASA).* https://www.ojp.gov/ncjrs/virtual-library/abstracts/behind-bars-ii-substance-abuse-and-americas-prison-population.

10 American Sociological Association. (2018, June 13). What is Sociology? *American Sociological Association.* https://www.asanet.org/about/what-is-sociology.

11 Center on the Developing Child at Harvard University. (2020b, October 30). What are ACEs? And How Do They Relate to Toxic Stress? Retrieved March 9, 2024 from https://developingchild.harvard.edu/resources/aces-and-toxic-stress-frequently-asked-questions/.

12 Joining Forces For Children. (2018, March 29). What are ACEs? Joining Forces For Children. Retrieved March 9, 2024 from https://www.joiningforcesforchildren.org/what-are-aces/.

13 Compassion Prison Project. (2024). Childhood Trauma Statistics. Compassion Prison Project. Retrieved March 9, 2024 from https://compassionprisonproject.org/childhood-trauma-statistics/.

14 Nembhard, S., and Lima, N. (2022, August 9). To Improve Safety, Understanding and Addressing the Link between Childhood Trauma and Crime Is Key. *The Urban Institute.* Retrieved March 10, 2024 from https://www.urban.org/urban-wire/improve-safety-understanding-and-addressing-link-between-childhood-trauma-and-crime-key.

15 The National Conference of State Legislatures. (2022, May 24). Racial and Ethnic Disparities in the Criminal Justice System. https://www.ncsl.org/research/civil-and-criminal-justice/racial-and-ethnic-disparities-in-the-criminal-justice-system.aspx.

16 The Sentencing Project. (2018, April 19). Report to the United Nations on Racial Disparities in the U.S. The Sentencing Project. https://www.sentencingproject.org/reports/report-to-the-united-nations-on-racial-disparities-in-the-u-s-criminal-justice-system.

17 Nembhard, S., and Robin, L. (2021, August). Racial and Ethnic Disparities throughout the Criminal Legal System. *The Urban Institute.* https://www.urban.org/sites/default/files/publications/104687/racial-and-ethnic-disparities-throughout-the-criminal-legal-system.pdf.

18 Hinton, E., Henderson, L., and Reed, C. (2018, May). An Unjust Burden: The Disparate Treatment of Black Americans in the Criminal Justice System. *The Vera Institute of Justice.* https://www.vera.org/publications/for-the-record-unjust-burden.

19 U.S. Census Bureau Quickfacts. (n.d.). Population Estimates, July 1, 2024, (V2024). *The U.S. Department of Commerce.* Retrieved January 3, 2025 from https://www.census.gov/quickfacts/.

20 See Note #4.

21 Eppler-Epstein, S., Gurvis, A., and King, R. (2016, December). The Alarming Lack of Data on Latinos in the Criminal Justice System. *The Urban Institute.* https://justiceroundtable.org/resource/the-alarming-lack-of-data-on-latinos-in-the-criminal-justice-system.

22 U.S. Department of Justice, Federal Bureau of Investigation. (n.d.). Crime in the United States 2019. FBI-UCR Program. Retrieved January 12, 2025 from https://ucr.fbi.gov/crime-in-the-u.s/2019/crime-in-the-u.s.-2019/tables/table-43A.

23 Noe-Bustamante, L., Gonzalez-Barrera, A., Edwards, K., Mora, L., and Lopez, M.H. (2021, November 4). Measuring the Racial Identity of Latinos. *Pew Research Center.* https://www.pewresearch.org/hispanic/2021/11/04measuring-the-racial-identity-of-latinos.

24 U.S. Department of Justice, Bureau of Justice Statistics. (2023, September). Prisons Report Series: Preliminary Data Release. (NJC number 307411). Retrieved January 25, 2024 from https://bjs.ojp.gov/library/pulications/prisons-report-series-preliminary-data-release.

25 U.S. Census Bureau. (n.d.). About the Decennial Census of Population and Housing. *U.S. Department of Commerce.* Retrieved January 12, 2025 from https://www.census.gov/programs-surveys/decennial-census/about.html#.

26 Alexander, M. (2012). *The New Jim Crow: Mass Incarceration in the Age of Colorblindness.* The New Press.

27 Mayo Clinic Staff. (2023, February 24). Antisocial Personality Disorder-Diagnosis and Treatment. *Mayo Clinic.* https://www.mayoclinic.org/diseases-conditions/antisocial-personality-disorder/diagnosis-treatment/drc-20353934.

28 National Institute on Drug Abuse. (2020, July 10). The Science of Addiction Treatment and Recovery. *National Institute on Drug Abuse.* https://nida.nih.gov/publications/drugs-brains-behavior-science-addiction/treatment-recovery.

Chapter 2

1 International Student. (2023). What Is Criminal Justice? in the US. *International Student.* Retrieved January 30, 2024 from https://www.international student.com/study-criminal-and-forensic-science/what-is-criminal-justice.

2 Cocklin, K.R. (1977). *Functions of Criminal Justice-Procedures, Tasks and Personnel* (from Fundamentals of Criminal Justice—A Syllabus and Workbook, 1977, 2nd Ed., By Dae H. Chang-See NCJ-44045). U.S. Department of Justice. Paladin House Publishers.

3 Dictionary.com. (n.d.). Police. *Dictionary.com.* Retrieved January 12, 2024 from https://www.dictionary.com/browse/police.

4 Balko, R. (2020, June 10). There's Racial Bias in Our Police Systems. *The Washington Post.* https://www.washingtonpost.com/grahics/2020/opinions/systemic-racism-police-evidence-criminal-justice-system/.

5 Pierson, E., Simoiu, C., Overgoor, J., et al. (2020). A Large-scale Analysis of Racial Disparities in Police Stops Across the United States. *Nature Human Behaviour* 4, 736–45. https://doi.org/10.1038/s41562-020-0858-1.

6 Stout, M. (2017, August 8). *Racial and Ethnic Disparities in Traffic Stops and Stop Outcomes in Springfield, Missouri: 2012–2016.* City of Springfield, MO. https://www.springfieldmo.gov/DocumentCenter/View/45970/Racial-and-Ethnic-Diparity-in-Traffic-Stops-Report-2012-2016.

7 CliffsNotes. (2024). *Police Brutality.* 2024 Course Hero, Inc. Retrieved January 30, 2024 from https://www.cliffsnotes.com/study-guides/criminal-justice/police-problems/police-brutality.

8 Hill, R. (2017, February 3). Understanding Five Different Types of Police Brutality. *Criminal Defense Blog.* https://criminallaw.com/lawyer/rhonda-b-hill-chicago-il/blog/understanding-five-different-types-of-police-brutality.

9 Peeples, L. (2020, June 19; Update 2021, May 26). What the Data Say About Police Brutality and Racial Bias—and Which Reforms Might Work. *Nature.com.* https://www.nature.com/articles/d41586-020-01846-z.

10 Edwards, F., Lee, H., and Esposito, M. (2019, August 20). Risk of Being Killed by Police Use of Force in the United States by Age, Race-Ethnicity, and Sex. *Proceedings of the National Academy of Sciences of the United States of America* 116 (34): 16793–8. https://pubmed.ncbi.nlm.nih.gov/31383756/.

11 Nix, J., Campbell, B.A., Byers, E.H., and Alpert, G.P. (2017, February 8). A Bird's Eye View of Civilians Killed by Police in 2015. *Criminology & Public Policy* 16 (1): 309–40. https://doi.org/10.1111/1745-9133.12269.

12 Abrams, Z. (2020, October 1). What Works to Reduce Police Brutality. *APA Monitor* 51 (7): 30. https://www.apa.org/monitor/2020/10/cover-police-brutality.

13 Pappas, S. (2020, June 4). How to Actually Stop Police Brutality, According to Science. *Live Science.* https://www.livescience.com/evidence-police-brutality-reform.html.

14 Wood, G., Tyler, T.R., and Papachristos, A.V. (2020, April 20; corrected 2021, July 6). Procedural Justice Training Reduces Police Use of Force and Complaints Against Officers. *Proceedings of the National Academy of Sciences of the United States of America.*

15 Schaeffer, J. (2024). U.S. Federal Courts 101. *Constitutional Accountability Center.* https://www.theusconstitution.org/u-s-federal-courts-101/.

16 Singh, A., and Corriher, B. (2016, August 8). State or Federal Court? *Center for American Progress.* Retrieved February 1, 2024 from https://www.americanprogress.org/article/fact-sheet-state-or-federal-court/.

17 Lesh, E. (2016, July 25). Justice Out of Balance. State Courts 101: Structure and Selection. *Lambda Legal*, 5. https://www.lambdalegal.org/node/42666.

18 Neily, C. (2019, August 8). Prisons are Packed Because Prosecutors are Coercing Plea Deals. And, Yes, It's Totally Legal. *NBC Universal.* https://www.nbcnews.com/think/opinion/prisons-are-packed-because-prosecutors-are-coercing-plea-deals-yes-ncna1034201.

19 CliffsNotes. (2024). The Process of Criminal Justice. *2024 Course Hero.* Retrieved February 2, 2024 from https://www.cliffsnotes.com/study-guides/criminal-justice/the-criminal-justice-system/the-process-of-criminal-justice.

20 Barrett, S. (n.d.). How Does a Criminal Case Go Through the Justice System? *AllLaw.* Retrieved February 2, 2024 from https://www.alllaw.com/articles/nolo/criminal/process.html.

21 APA's Committee on Legal Issues. (2016, July/August). Protecting Patient Privacy When the Court Calls. *APA Monitor* 47 (7): 64. Retrieved April 20, 2024 from https://www.apa.org/monitor/2016/07-08/ce-corner.

22 Subramanian, R., Digard, L., Washington II, M., and Sorage, S. (2020, September). *In the Shadows: A Review of the Research on Plea Bargaining.* New York: Vera Institute of Justice. https://www.vera.org/publications/in-the-shadows-plea-bargaining.

23 Stohr, M., Walsch, A., and Hemmens, C. (2008). *Corrections: A Text/Reader.* Sage, 1. ISBN 978-1-4129-3733-3. Retrieved February 3, 2024 from https://edge.sagepub.com/stohr3e.

24 Belcher, E. (n.d.). *New York Prisons and Jails: Historical Research: Definitions: Jail & Prison.* John Jay College of Criminal Justice, CUNY/LibGuides. https://guides.lib.jjay.cuny.edu/NYPrisons.

25 The Free Dictionary. (n.d.). Jail. *The Free Dictionary.com.* Retrieved February 3, 2024 from https://legal-dictionary.thefreedictionary.com/Jail.

26 Cambridge University Press. (n.d.). Electronic-Monitoring. *Cambridge Dictionary.* Retrieved February 3, 2024 from https://dictionary.cambridge.org/us/dictionary/english/electronic-monitoring.

27 American Bar Association. (2021, December 30). How Courts Work. https://www.americanbar.org/groups/public_education/resources/law_related_education_network/how_courts_work.

28 The Free Dictionary. (n.d.). Restitution. *The Free Dictionary.com*. Retrieved February 4, 2024 from https://www.thefreedictionary.com/restitution.

29 The Free Dictionary. (n.d.). Fines. *The Free Dictionary.com*. Retrieved February 4, 2024 from https://www.thefreedictionary.com/fine.

30 The Free Dictionary. Restorative Justice. *The Free Dictionary.com*. Retrieved February 4, 2024 from https://www.thefreedictionary.com/restorative+justice.

31 Delaney, R., Subramanian, R., Shames, A., and Turner, N. (2018, September). Examining Prisons Today. *The Vera Institute of Justice*. https://www.vera.org/reimagining-prison-web-report/examining-prisons-today.

32 Mental Health America. (n.d.). Position Statement 56: Mental Health Treatment in Correctional Facilities. *Mental Health America*. Retrieved February 4, 2024 from https://www.mhanational.org/issues/position-statement-56-mental-health-treatment-correctional-facilities.

33 Hager, E., Rich, G., and Meagher, T. (2015, June 5). Job Opening: No Training, Low Pay, High Turnover. *The Marshall Project*. https://www.themarshallproject.org/2015/06/05/job-opening-no-training-low-pay-high-turnover.

Chapter 3

1 Correctional Officer.org (n.d.). What Are the Duties of a Correctional Officer? *Correctional Officer.org*. Retrieved February 6, 2024 from https://www.correctionalofficer.org/faq/correctional-officer-job-description.

2 Farkas, M.A. (2000). A Typology of Correctional Officers. *International Journal of Offender Therapy and Comparative Criminology* 44 (4): 431–49. https://doi.org/10.1177/0306624X00444003.

3 King, M.M., and Labrecque, R.M. (2017, January). American Prisons and Jails: An Encyclopedia of Controversies and Trends. *ABC-CLIO*. Editors: Worley, V.B., and Worley, R.M. Typology of Correctional Officers. https://www.researchgate.net/publication/311984265.

4 Merriam-Webster. (n.d.). Authoritarian. *Merriam-Webster.com Dictionary*. Retrieved February 6, 2024 from https://www.merriam-webster.com/dictionary/authoritarian.

5 Dictionary.com. (n.d.). Authoritarian. *Dictionary.com*. Retrieved February 6, 2024 from https://www.dictionary.com/browse/authoritarian.

6 American Psychological Association (APA) Dictionary of Psychology. (Updated 2018, April 19). Reactance Theory. *APA Dictionary of Psychology*. Retrieved February 9, 2024 from https://dictionary.apa.org/reactance-theory.

7 Brehm, S.S. (1981, September). Psychological Reactance and the Attractiveness of Unattainable Objects: Sex Differences in Children's Responses to an Elimination of Freedom. *Sex Roles* 7: 937–49. https://doi.org/10.1007/BF00290976.

8 Silvia, P.J. (2005). Deflecting Reactance: The Role of Similarity in Increasing Compliance and Reducing Resistance. *Basic and Applied Social Psychology* 27 (3): 277–84. https://doi.org/10.1207/s15324834basp2703_9.

9 Miller, C.H., Burgoon, M., Grandpre, J.R., and Alvaro, E.M. (2006). Identifying Principal Risk Factors for the Initiation of Adolescent Smoking Behaviors: The Significance of Psychological Reactance. *Health Communication* 19 (3): 241–52. https://doi.org/10.1207/s15327027hc1903_6.

10 Black, D.W., Gunter, T., Loveless, P., Allen, J., and Sieleni, B. (2010, May 22). Antisocial Personality Disorder in Incarcerated Offenders: Psychiatric Comorbidity and Quality of Life. *Annals of Clinical Psychiatry: Official Journal of the American Academy of Clinical Psychiatrists* 2: 113–20. https://pubmed.ncbi.nlm.nih.gov/20445838/.

11 Seemann, E. (2003). *Personality Style and Psychological Reactance: Theory Confirmation and Empirical Prediction of Reactant Personalities*. Doctoral Dissertation. Louisiana Tech. https://digitalcommons.latech.edu/cgi/viewcontent.cgi?params=/context/dissertations/article/1653/&path_info=Personality_style_and_psycholo.pdf.

12 Merriam-Webster. (n.d.). Rehabilitation. *Merriam-Webster.com Dictionary*. Retrieved February 8, 2024 from https://www.merriam-webster.com/dictionary/rehabilitation.

13 Prochaska, J.O., DiClemente, C.C., and Norcross, J.C. (1992). In Search of How People Change: Applications to Addictive Behaviors. *American Psychologist* 47 (9): 1102–14. https://doi.org/10.1037//0003-066x.47.9.1102.

14 LaMorte, W.W. (2022, November 3). Behavioral Change Models. The Transtheoretical Model (Stages of Change). https://sphweb.bumc.bu.edu/otlt/mphmodules/sb/behavioralchangetheories/behavioralchangetheories6.html.

Chapter 4

1 Cambridge English Dictionary. (n.d.). Prison Warden. *Cambridge English Dictionary*. Retrieved March 28, 2024 from https://dictionary.cambridge.org/us/dictionary/english/prison-warden.

2 Federal Bureau of Prisons. BOP: Jobs. (n.d.). Work on the Inside. *Federal Bureau of Prisons. BOP: Jobs*. Retrieved April 3, 2024 from https://www.bop.gov/jobs.

3 United States Courts. (n.d.). Probation and Pretrial Officers and Officer Assistants. *United States Courts*. Retrieved April 6, 2024 from https://www.uscourts.gov/services-forms/probation-and-pretrial-services/probation-and-pretrial-officers-and-officer.

4 Myers, L. (2024, March 11). The Courtroom: Breaking Down the Jobs. https://www.northwestcareercollege.edu/blog/the-courtoom-breaking-down-the-jobs/.

5 CorrectionalOfficer.org. (n.d.). How to Become a Prison Warden. *CorrectionalOfficer.org*. Retrieved April 13, 2024 from https://www.correctionalofficer.org/career/prison-warden.

6 All Criminal Justice Schools. (n.d.). Is a Correctional Administration Career Right for You? *All Criminal Justice Schools*. Retrieved April 13, 2024 from https://www.allcriminaljusticeschools.com/specialties/correctional-administration/.

7 CorrectionalOfficerEDU.org. (n.d.). Corrections Officer Training. *CorrectionalOfficerEDU.org*. Retrieved April 14, 2024 from https://www.correctionalofficeredu.org/training/.

8 CorrectionalOfficer.org. (n.d.). Becoming a Case Manager. *CorrectionalOfficer.org*. Retrieved April 25, 2024 from https://www.correctionalofficer.org/career/case-manager.

9 Federal Bureau of Prisons. (n.d.). BOP: Secretary. Job Series Number: 0318. *Federal Bureau of Prisons*. Retrieved April 26, 2024 from https://www.bop.gov/jobs/positions/index.jsp?p=Secretary.

10 State of Colorado CDOC-Librarian II (Denver) (2023). *Job Bulletin*. Denver, CO. Retrieved April 27, 2024 from https://www.governmentjobs.com/careers/colorado/jobs/newprint/4175439.

11 State of Colorado CDOC-Physician (Colorado) (2024). *Job Bulletin*. Colorado. Retrieved April 28, 2024 from https://www.governmentjobs.com/careers/colorado/jobs/4392253/cdoc-physician.

12 Deshaies, S. (2023, January 11). How to Become a Correctional Nurse. *NurseJournal*. Retrieved April 29, 2024 from https://noursejournal.org/careers/correctional-nurse/how-to-become/.

13 ECPI University. (n.d.). What's It Like to Work in a Correctional Facility as an EMT? Emergency Medicine in Correctional Facilities. *ECPI Blog*. Retrieved April 29, 2024 from https://www.ecpi.edu/blog/what-is-it-like-to-work-in-a-correctional-facility-as-an-emt.

14 Federal Bureau of Prisons. (n.d.). BOP: Dentist. Job Series Number: 0680. *Federal Bureau of Prisons*. Retrieved May 1, 2024 from https://www.bop.gov/jobs/positions/index.jsp?p=Dentist.

15 Federal Bureau of Prisons. (n.d.). BOP: Recreation Specialist. Job Series Number: 0188. *Federal Bureau of Prisons*. Retrieved May 4, 2024 from https://www.bop.gov/jobs/positions/index.jsp?p=Recreation%20Specialist.

16 Federal Bureau of Prisons. (n.d.). BOP: Chaplain. Job Series Number: 0060. *Federal Bureau of Prisons*. Retrieved May 4, 2024 from https://www.bop.gov/jobs/positions/index.jsp?p=Chaplain.

17 Federal Bureau of Prisons. (n.d.). BOP: Maintenance Mechanic. Job Series Number: 4749. *Federal Bureau of Prisons*. Retrieved May 5, 2024 from https://www.bop.gov/jobs/positions/index.jsp?p=Maintenence%20Mechanic.

18 Federal Bureau of Prisons. (n.d.). BOP: Food Service Supervisor. Job Series Number: 7400. *Federal Bureau of Prisons*. Retrieved May 5, 2024 from https://www.bop.gov/jobs/positions/index.jsp?p=Food%20Service%20Supervisor.

19 CorrectionalOfficer.org. (n.d.). Becoming a Community Corrections Officer. *CorrectionalOfficer.org*. Retrieved May 6, 2024 from https://www.correctionalofficer.org/career/community-corrections-officer.

20 Federal Bureau of Prisons. (n.d.). BOP: Education. Education Programs. *Federal Bureau of Prisons*. Retrieved May 7, 2024 from https://www.bop.gov/inmates/custody_and_care/education.jsp.

21 Indeed Editorial Team. (Updated 2022, June 24). How to Become a Vocational Counselor (With Steps). *Indeed Career Guide*. Retrieved May 7, 2024 from https://www.indeed.com/career-advice/finding-a-job/how-to-become-a-vocational-counselor.

22 Criminal Justice Degree Schools Staff Writers. (Updated 2020, October 15). How to Become a Parole Officer. Parole Officer: Career Guide. *Criminal Justice Degree Schools*. Retrieved May 7, 2024 from https://www.criminaljusticedegreeschools.com/careers/parole-officer.

23 Criminal Justice Degree Schools Staff Writers. (Updated 2020, October 15). Probation Officer Career. Probation Officer: Career Guide. *Criminal Justice Degree Schools*. Retrieved May 7, 2024 from https://www.criminaljusticedegreeschools.com/careers/probation-officer.

24 International Association of Chiefs of Police. (n.d.). Basic Requirements—Discover Policing. Discover Policing. *International Association of Chiefs of Police*. Retrieved May 10, 2024 from https://www.discoverpolicing.org/about-policing/basic-requirements.

25 Police 1 Staff. (2024, April 29). What to Expect from Police Academy Training. Police 1. *Lexipol Media Group*. https://www.police1.com/how-to-become-a-police-officer/articles/what-to-expect-from-police-academy-training-TphD8qpkqgg68nYc/.

26 The Supreme Court of the United States. (n.d.). FAQs—General Information. The Supreme Court of the United States. Retrieved May 12, 2024 from https://www

.supremecourt.gov/about/faq_general.aspx#:~:text=Do%20you%20have%20to%20be,been%20trained%20in%20the%20law.

27 Ebadolahi, M. (2018, August 30). How Do I Become a Judge? *BarMax*. Retrieved May 15, 2024 from https://testmaxprep.com/blog/bar-exam/how-to-become-a-judge.

28 National University. (n.d.). *How to Become a Paralegal*. National University. Retrieved May 19, 2024 from https://www.nu.19.

29 CorrectionalOfficer.org. (n.d.). How to Become a Bailiff. *CorrectionalOfficer.org*. Retrieved May 6, 2024 from https://www.correctionalofficer.org/career/paralegal.

30 National Center for State Courts. (n.d.). Court Interpreter Resources. *National Center for State Courts*. Retrieved on May 21, 2024 from https://www.ncsc.org/education-and-careers/state-interpreter-certification.

31 Language Connections Interpreter Training Programs. (n.d.). What are the Requirements to Be a Legal or a Court Interpreter? *Language Connections Interpreter Training Programs*. Retrieved May 22, 2024 from https://interpretertrain.com/what-are-the-requirements-to-be-a-legal-or-a-court-interpreter.

32 Beltrani, A. (2023, October 10). Unlocking Wellness Behind the Bars: Illuminating the Struggles and Triumphs of Mental Health in Prisons. *Concept: Continuing & Professional Studies*. Palo Alto University. https://concept.paloaltou.edu/resources/business-of-practice-blog/unlocking-wellness-behind-the-bars.

33 CorrectionalOfficerEDU.org. (n.d.). Corrections Officer Training. *CorrectionalOfficerEDU.org*. Retrieved May 27, 2024 from https://www.correctionalofficeredu.org/training/.

34 National Commission on Correctional Health Care. (n.d.). Mental Health Training for Correctional Officers. *National Commission on Correctional Health Care*. Retrieved May 30, 2024 from https://www.ncchc.org/q-a/mental-health-training-for-correctional-officers/.

35 U.S. Department of Justice. (n.d.). Training. Police—Mental Health Collaboration (PMHC) Toolkit. Crisis Intervention Team Training. Mental Health First Aid For Public Safety. Bureau of Justice Assistance. *U.S. Department of Justice*. Retrieved June 1, 2024 from https://bja.ojp.gov/program/pmhc/training.

36 Butterworth, L. (2022, July 7; Updated 2024, October 5). What is Empathy Training? *Empathy First*. https://www.empathyfirst.com.au/post/what-is-empathy-training.

37 Multnomah County. (n.d.). EPICS. *Department of Community Justice*. Retrieved August 1, 2025 from https://share.google/3lhywcYFiell8XA2M.

38 United States Department of Justice. (n.d.). Mission. National Initiative for Building Community Trust & Justice. *Office of Justice Programs, United States Department of Justice*. Retrieved June 26, 2024 from https://trustandjustice.org/about/mission.

39 Weisburd, D., Telep, C.W., Vovak, H., Zastrow, T., Braga, A.A., and Turchan, B. (2022, March 28). Reforming the Police Through Procedural Justice Training: A Multicity Randomized Trial at Crime Hot Spots. *Proceedings of the National Academy of Sciences of the United States of America* 119 (14): e2118780119. https://www.pnas.org/doi/full/10.1073/pnas.2118780119.

40 Fiske, Z.R., Songer, D.M., and Schriver, J.L. (2021, June). A National Survey of Police Mental Health Training. *Journal of Police and Criminal Psychology* 36 (2): 236–42. https://www.researchgate.net/publication/343108149.

41 Darani, S.A., McMaster, R., Wolff, E., Bonato, S., Simpson, A.S., Glancy, G., Sandhu, K., and Quinn, J. (2023, March 16). Addressing the Mental Health Needs of Inmates Through Education for Correctional Officers—A Narrative Review. *Journal of Continuing Education in the Health Professions*. https://www.semanticscholor.org/paper/Addressing-the-Mental-Health-Needs-of-Inmates-for-Darani-McMaster/dc877b62b5d70ab7824a601e58bf41e63b88614a.

42 Vera Institute of Justice. (n.d.). The Prison Experience for Corrections Staff. *Vera Institute of Justice*. Retrieved on June 5, 2024 from https://www.vera.org/reimagining-prison-web-report/examining-prisons-today/the-prison-experience-for-corrections-staff.

43 Otto, H.D., and Gatens, A. (2022, May 24). Understanding Police Officer Stress: A Review of the Literature. *Illinois Criminal Justice Information Authority*. https://icjia.illinois.gov/researchhub/articles/understanding-police-officer-stress-a-review-of-the-literature.

44 London: National Institute for Health and Care Excellence (NICE). (2017, March). *National Guideline Alliance (UK). Mental Health of Adults in Contact with the Criminal Justice System: Identification and Management of Mental Health Problems and Integration of Care for Adults in Contact with the Criminal Justice System*. London: National Institute for Health and Care Excellence (NICE); (Nice Guideline, No. 66.) 4, Staff Training. https://www.ncbi.nlm.nih.gov/books/NBK533143/.

Chapter 5

1 Raven, B.H. (1965). Social Influence and Power. *Current Studies in Social Psychology*. Editors: Steiner, I.D., and Fishbein, M. 371–82.

2 Kovach, M. (2020). Leader Influence: A Research Review of French and Raven's (1959) Power Dynamics. *The Journal of Values-Based Leadership* 13 (2): Article 15. https://doi.org/10.22543/0733.132.1312.

3 Mind Tools Content Team. (n.d.). French and Raven's Five Forms of Power. *Mind Tools*. Retrieved July 22, 2024 from https://www.mindtools.com/abwzix3/french-and-ravens-five-forms-of-power.

4 Stiener, B., and Wooldredge, J. (2018, August 7). Prison Officer Legitimacy, Their Exercise of Power, and Inmate Rule Breaking. *Criminology and Criminal Justice Faculty Publications* 31. https://digitalcommons.unomaha.edu/criminaljusticefacpub/31/.

5 Ferdik, F.V., and Smith, H.P. (2015, September). Maximum Security Correctional Officers: An Exploratory Investigation Into Their Social Bases of Power. *American Journal of Criminal Justice* 41 (3). doi: 10.1007/s12103-015-9307-5. https://www.researchgate.net/publication/282517904.

6 Applegate, B.K., Ouellette, H.M., and Wareham, J. (2023, September 13). Jail Officers' Adherence to Traditional Bases of Social Power: Understanding Inmate Control in a Unique Correctional Context. *The Prison Journal* 103 (2). doi: 1177/00328855231200637. https://journals.sagepub.com/doi/10.1177/00328855231200637.

7 See Note #4. Prison Officer Legitimacy, Their Exercise of Power, and Inmate Rule Breaking.

8 APA Dictionary of Psychology. (n.d.). Therapeutic Alliance. *APA Dictionary of Psychology*. Retrieved September 14, 2024 from https://dictionary.apa.org/therapeutic-alliance.

9 Ardito, R.B., and Rabellino, D. (2011, October 18). Therapeutic Alliance and Outcome of Psychotherapy: Historical Excursus, Measurements, and Prospects for Research. *Frontiers in Psychology* 2: 270. doi: 10.3389/fpsyg.2011.00270. PMID: 22028698; PMCID: PMC3198542. https://pmc.ncbi.nlm.nih.gov/articles/PMC3198542/.

10 See Note #9.

11 Blasko, B., Serran, G., and Abracen, J. (2018). The Role of the Therapeutic Alliance in Offender Therapy. *New Frontiers in Offender Treatment: The Translation of Evidence-Based Practices to Correctional Settings* (1st Edition). Editors: Jeglic, E.L., and Calkins, C. Springer, 87–108.

Chapter 6

1 Cherry, K. (2024, January 12). How Client-Centered Therapy Works? *Verywell Mind*. Retrieved January 26, 2024 from https://www.verywellmind.com/client-centered

-therapy2795999#:~:text=Client%2Dcentered%20therapy%2C%20also%20known,or%20offer%20suggestions%20or%20solutions.

2 THERAPlatform. (2024). Person Centered Therapy Techniques. *THERAPlatform.* https://www.theraplatform.com/blog/338/person-centered-therapy-techniques.

3 Petiprin, A. (2023). Robert R. Carkhuff. *Nursing Theory.* https://nursing-theory.org/nursing-theorists/Robert-Carkhuff.php.

4 Gibbard, I., and Hanley, T. (2008, November 17). A Five Year Evaluation of the Effectiveness of Person-centered Counselling in Routine Clinical Practice in Primary Care. *Counselling and Psychotherapy Research* 8 (4): 215–22. https://doi.org/10.1080/147331408023054.

5 Cooper, M. (2024). University of Roehampton. Retrieved January 26, 2024 from https://www.roehampton.ac.uk/staff/Mick-Cooper.

6 Cooper, M. (2019, July 2). Is Person-Centered Therapy Effective? The Facts. *Mick Cooper Training and Consultancy.* https://mick-cooper.squarespace.com/new-blog/2019/7/2/is-person-centered-therapy-effective-the-facts.

7 Stinson, J.D., and Clark, M.D. (2017). *Motivational Interviewing with Offenders, Engagement, Rehabilitation and Reentry.* The Guilford Press.

8 Miller, W.R., and Rollnick, S. (2013). *Motivational Interviewing: Helping People to Change* (3rd Edition). Guilford Press.

9 Miller, W.R., and Rollnick, S. (2009). Ten Things that MI Is Not. *Behavioral and Cognitive Psychotherapy* 37: 129–40.

10 Motivational Interviewing Network of Trainers. (2021). Understanding Motivational Interviewing. *Motivational Interviewing Network of Trainers.* https://motivationalinterviewing.org/understanding-motivational-interviewing.

11 Bandura, A. (1986). *Social Foundations of Thought and Action: A Social Cognitive Theory.* Prentice-Hall.

12 University of Massachusetts. (n.d.). Definition of Motivational Interviewing. [White paper]. Retrieved January 28, 2024 from https://umass.edu/studentlife/sites/default/files/documents/pdf/Motivational_Interviewing_Definition_Principles_Approach.pdf.

13 Lundahl, B.W., Kunz, C., Brownwell, C., Tollefson, D., and Burke, B.L. (2010). A Meta-Analysis of Motivational Interviewing: Twenty-Five Years of Empirical Studies. *Research on Social Welfare Practice* 20 (2): 137–60.

14 American Psychological Association. (2017). What is Cognitive Behavioral Therapy? *American Psychological Association.* https://www.apa.org/ptsd-guideline/patients-and-families/cognitive-behavioral.

15 See Note #14.

16 Lipsey, M., Landenberger, N., and Wilson, S. (2007, August 13). *Effects of Cognitive-Behavioral Programs for Criminal Offenders*. Wiley. https://onlinelibrary.wiley.com/doi/full/10.4073/csr.2007.6.

17 (2017, November 7). Assessing Risk and Needs: What is the LSI-R? *Geo Reentry Services*. Retrieved August 20, 2025 from https://www.georeentry.com/assessing-risk-needs-lsi-r/.

18 American Psychological Association (APA) Dictionary of Psychology. (n.d.). Suggestion. *APA Dictionary of Psychology*. Retrieved February 7, 2024 from https://dictionary.apa.org/suggestion.

19 American Psychological Association (APA) Dictionary of Psychology. (n.d.). Placebo. *APA Dictionary of Psychology*. Retrieved February 7, 2024 from https://dictionary.apa.org/placebo.

20 Michael, R.B., Garry, M., and Kirsch, I. (2012, May 30). Suggestion, Cognition, and Behavior. *Sage Journals. Current Directions in Psychological Science* 21 (3). https://cdp.sagepub.com/content/21/3/151.

21 Mo, Q., Qiu, R., Cheng, S., Chen, X., and Peng, A. (2022). Positive Psychological Suggestions Improve the Self-efficacy, Social Functioning and Mood of Patients Undergoing Replantation. https://www.ncbi.nlm.nih.gov/pmc/articles/PMC9360848.

22 Hui, B.P.H., Ng, J.C.K., Berzaghi, E., Cunningham-Amos, L.A., and Kogan, A. (2020, December). Rewards of Kindness? A Meta-Analysis of the Link Between Prosociality and Well-Being. *Psychological Bulletin* 146 (12): 1084–116. https://pubmed.ncbi.nlm.nih.gov/32881540/.

23 Gallo, A. (2017, December 1). How to Control Your Emotions During a Difficult Conversation. *Harvard Business Review*. https://hbr.org/2017/12/how-to-control-your-emotions-during-a-difficult-conversation.

24 Mayo Clinic Staff. (2020, May 29). Being Assertive: Reduce Stress, Communicate Better. *Mayo Clinic*. https://www.mayoclinic.org/healthy-lifestyle/stress-management/in-depth/assertive/art-20044644.

25 Asensio, S., Hernandez-Rabaza, V., and Semper, J.V.O. (2020, April 21). What is the "Trigger" of Addiction? National Library of Medicine. *NCBI*. https://www.ncbi.nlm.nih.gov/pmc/articles/PMC7186308/.

26 National Wellness Institute. (2023). The Six Dimensions of Wellness. *National Wellness Institute*. https://nationalwellness.org/resources/six-dimensions-of-wellness.

27 Harvard Health Publishing. (2020, July 6). *Understanding the Stress Response*. Harvard Health Publishing. Retrieved March 3, 2024 from https://www.health.harvard.edu/staying-healthy/understanding-the-stress-response.

28 Office for Victims of Crime Training & Technical Assistance Center. (2022, July 28). Victim Impact: Listen and Learn. *Office for Victims of Crime Training & Technical Assistance Center*. https://www.ovcttac.gov/victimimpact/.

29 Psychology Today. (2024). Mindfulness. *Psychology Today*. Retrieved January 29, 2024 from https://www.psychologytoday.com/us/basics/mindfulness.

30 health.ucdavis.edu. (2022, December 14). 10 Health Benefits of Meditation and How to Focus on Mindfulness. *Ucdavishealth Mental Health. Cultivating Health*. https://share.google/FAGG9haXNAqHKe5mv.

31 Davis, T. (2020, December 3). What Is Positive Thinking? +9 Examples of Positive Thoughts. *PositivePsychology.com. Optimism & Mindset*. https://share.google/D6Toos9NXocEKJmf8.

32 Salamon, M. (2024, September 11). *Gratitude Enhances Health, Brings Happiness—and May Even Lengthen Lives*. Harvard Health Publishing. Mind & Mood. https://share.google/P9um8JErhwGhrGfhF.

33 Glicksman, E. (2019, May). Physical Discipline Is Harmful and Ineffective. *American Psychological Association. Monitor* 50 (5): 22. https://www.apa.org/monitor/2019/05/physical-discipline.

34 Dictionary.com. (n.d.). Role Model. *Dictionary.com*. Retrieved January 29, 2024 from https://www.dictionary.com/browse/role-model.

Chapter 7

1 Okonofua, J.A., Saadatian, K., Ocampo, J., Ruiz, M., and Oxholm, P.D. (2021, April 6). A Scalable Empathic Supervision Intervention to Mitigate Recidivism From Probation and Parole. *Proceedings of the National Academy of Sciences of the United States of America* 118 (14): e2018036118. doi: 10.1073/pnas.2018036118. PMID: 33782121; PMCID: PMC8040791. https://pubmed.ncbi.nlm.nih.gov/33782121/.

2 Hachtel, H., Vogel, T., and Huber, C.G. (2019, April 12). Mandated Treatment and Its Impact on Therapeutic Process and Outcome Factors. *Front Psychiatry* 10: 219. doi: 10.3389/fpsyt.2019.00219. PMID: 31031658; PMCID: PMC6474319. https://www.ncbi.nlm.nih.gov/pmc/articles/PMC6474319/.

3 See Chapter 6, Note #13.

4 Taxman, F.S., Walters, S.T., Sloas, L.B., Lerch, J., and Rodriguez, M. (2015, July). Motivational Tools to Improve Probationer Treatment Outcomes. *Contemporary Clinical Trials* 43: 120–8. doi: 10.1016/j.cct.2015.05.016. Epub 2015 May 22.

PMID: 26009023; PMCID: PMC4522391. https://ncbi.nlm.nih.gov/pmc/articles/PMC4522391.

5 See Chapter 6, Note #16.

6 Hull, O.J., Breckler, O.D., and Jaegers, L.A. (2023, June). Integrated Safety and Health Promotion Among Correctional Workers and People Incarcerated: A Scoping Review. *International Journal of Environmental Research and Public Health* 20 (12): 6104. doi: 10.3390/ijerph20126104. PMID: 37372691; PMCID: PMC 10298485. https://pmc.ncbi.nlm.nih.gov/articles/PMC10298485.

7 Martinez-Inigo, D. (2021, October). The Role of Prison Officers' Regulation of Inmates' Affect on Their Exposure to Violent Behaviors and the Development of PTSD Symptoms. *European Journal of Psychotraumatology* 12 (1): 1956126. doi: 10.1080/20008198.2021.1956126. PMID: 34691368; PMCID: PMC8530476. https://pubmed.ncbi.nlm.nih.gov/34691368/.

8 Aronov-Jacoby, S. (2022, January 27). The Benefits of Self-Awareness. *Humber River Health News.* https://www.hrh.ca/2022/01/27/the-benefits-of-self-awareness/.

9 Gangi, A. (2015, September 22). Why It's OK to be Empathic Toward Inmates. *Corrections 1.* Retrieved January 15, 2025 from https://www.corrections1.com/corrections-training/articles/why-its-ok-to-be-empathic-toward-inmates-R9HKu2ynUWd1z5ao/.

10 See Note #6.

11 See Chapter 6, Note #16.

12 Toler, D., and Boone, R. (2022, August 22). Reducing Recidivism Through Corrections and Workforce Partnerships. *Corrections 1.* https://www.corrections1.com/re-entry-and-recidivism/articles/reducing-recidivism-through-corrections-and-workforce-partnerships-51Vy80VAa03lrcAK/.

13 Zuzek-Arden, T., and Boison, G. (2021, March 26). Data Can Help Reduce Recidivism and Reform Criminal Justice. *BCG.* https://www.bcg.com/publications/2021/reducing-recidivism-using-data.

14 Visher, C., and Eason, J. (2021, April). A Better Path Forward for Criminal Justice: Changing Prisons to Help People Change. *Brookings.* https://www.brookings.edu/articles/a-better-path-forward-for-criminal-justice-changing-prisons-to-help-people-change.

15 Prison Policy Initiative. (n.d.). Economics of Incarceration: The Economic Drivers and Consequences of Mass Incarceration. *Prison Policy Initiative.* Retrieved November 16, 2024 from https://www.prisonpolicy.org/research/economics_of_incarceration.

16 Hendrickson, C., and Delaney, R. (2012, January). Price of Prisons: What Incarceration Costs Taxpayers. *NCJRS Virtual Library.* Retrieved November 16,

2024 from https://www.ojp.gov/ncjrs/virtual-library/abstacts/price-prisons-what-incarceration-costs-taxpayers.

17 Knapp, M., and Wong, G. (2023, March 4). Economic Evaluations of Mental Health Interventions in Criminal Justice. *Criminal Behaviour & Mental Health* 33 (2): 139–48. https://doi.org/10.1002/cbm.2286.

18 Clark, P. (2010, May 28). Archived Preventing Future Crime With Cognitive Behavioral Therapy. *National Institute of Justice.* nij.ojp.gov: Retrieved November 17, 2024 from https://nij.ojp.gov/topics/articles/preventing-future-crime-cognitive-behavioral-therapy.

19 National Alliance on Mental Health. (n.d.). Mental Health Treatment While Incarcerated. *National Alliance on Mental Health.* Retrieved on November 17, 2024 from https://www.nami.org/advocay/policy-priorities/improving-health/mental-health-treatment-while-incarcerated.

20 See Chapter 4, Note #37.

Chapter 8

1 NCRP National Committee for Responsive Philanthropy. (2024). Key Terms for Understanding Criminal Justice Reform. *NCRP National Committee for Responsive Philanthropy.* Retrieved December 5, 2024 from https://ncrp.org/resources/key-terms-for-understanding-criminal-justice-reform.

2 Downes-Le Guin, I., and Young, D. (Updated: 2023, November 21). Prison Reform History, Facts & Importance. *Study.com.* Retrieved December 7, 2024 from https://study.com/acadamy/lesson/prison-reform-history-issues-movement.html.

3 Congressional Black Caucus Foundation, Inc. (CBC). (n.d.). History. Finding Justice within America's Criminal Justice System. *Avoice Web Site.* Retrieved December 7, 2024 from https://avoice.cbcfinc.org/exhibits/criminal-justice/history.

4 Office of Justice Programs. (2024, April 30). Impacts of the Second Chance Act. Office of Justice Programs. *United States Department of Justice.* https://ojp.gov/safe-communities/from-the-vault/impacts-second-chance-act.

5 Subramanian, R., and Arzy, L. (2021, May 21). State Policing Reforms Since George Floyd's Murder. *Brennan Center for Justice.* Retrieved December 7, 2024 from https://www.brennancenter.org/our-work/research-reports/state-policing-reforms-george-floyds-murder.

6 See Chapter 7, Note #19.

7 See Chapter 6, Note #1.

INDEX

ABOUT THE AUTHOR

Howie Schweber, MA, CAS, LPC is a Colorado Licensed Professional Counselor, Colorado Certified Addiction Specialist, and Colorado Department of Corrections Approved Treatment Provider. Howie facilitated individual and group substance use disorder, mental health, and didactic therapy in Colorado justice system halfway houses for over twenty-five years and has been in private practice for more than forty years. In private practice, Howie specializes in substance use disorder, depression, anxiety, justice system involvement, and anger management, and provides individual and couples counseling for adults. Howie's treatment philosophy emphasizes client-centered and cognitive behavioral psychotherapies and utilizes motivational interviewing techniques. Howie is a member of the American Counseling Association.